From Forecastle to Cabin

FROM FORECASTLE TO CABIN

Captain Samuel Samuels

Edited with an introduction by
Vincent McInerney

Seaforth
PUBLISHING

This edition copyright © A Vincent McInerney 2012

First published in Great Britain in 2012 by
Seaforth Publishing,
Pen & Sword Books Ltd,
47 Church Street,
Barnsley S70 2AS

www.seaforthpublishing.com

British Library Cataloguing in Publication Data
A catalogue record for this book
is available from the British Library
ISBN 978 1 84832 126 7

Typeset and designed by M.A.T.S. Leigh-on-Sea, Essex
Printed and bound in Great Britain
by CPI Group (UK) Ltd, Croydon, CR0 4YY

Contents

Contents

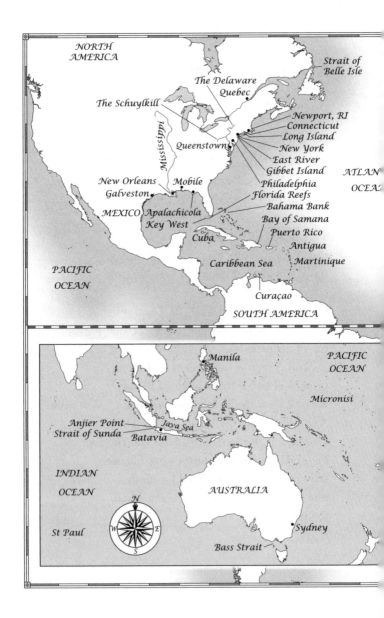

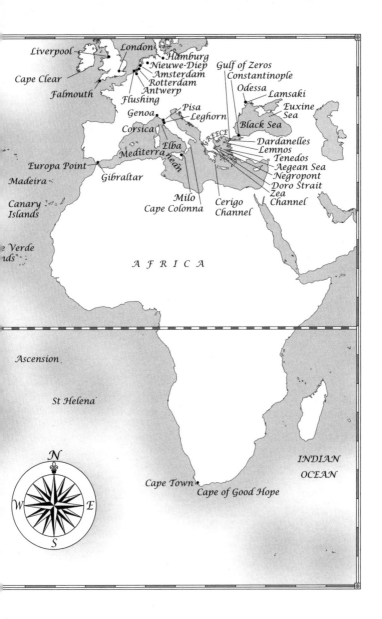

Editorial Note

THE TEXT USED is that of the Harper, New York edition of 1877, together with certain details of the Bloody Forties mutiny on the *Dreadnought* as contained in Lubbock's *Western Ocean Packets*[1] – Lubbock seemingly having access to a different account than that in the specified edition.

The word count has been reduced from approximately 80,000 to 45,000. Losses have been in some repetitious sailing passages, and in elaborate technical details relating to the handling of sails and rigging that tended to slow the narrative, and which may be of little interest to a contemporary reader.

Introduction

> Being impossible to sack a man at sea ... a mate has
> to depend on himself to see his orders obeyed with
> alacrity. This is better understood in American ships;
> where the chief quality looked for in an officer is a
> competent knowledge of how to knock a man down
> – then kick him for falling.[2]

THIS IS THE autobiography of an American who ran
away to sea at the age of eleven, and charts his rise from
the lowliest seaman (berthed under the forecastle) to
the command of his own ship and the occupation of the
luxurious after-cabin. In the course of an action-packed
career spanning half a century, Samuel Samuels experienced almost all of the vicissitudes of life in the
nineteenth-century merchant service: storm and shipwreck, famine and disease, press-gangs and desertion,
piracy, violence and mutiny – this last, at different
times, as both mutineer and victim. Like many a sailor
he was often in more danger ashore than afloat, but
many of his adventures make excellent stories – not
least his fairytale but foolhardy rescue of a Christian
woman from the harem in Constantinople. In this case

the story did not quite follow the conventional script, as our hero was a married man and the heroine wed his accomplice in the rescue.

Samuels is best known for his later career, as captain of the sailing packet *Dreadnought*, a ship built especially for him and under his direction. Known as the 'wild boat of the Atlantic' in the 1850s, this ship was reckoned the fastest sailing vessel on the New York-Liverpool service. This success was largely down to Samuels' hard-driving style as master, and much of the latter part of the book is taken up with the resulting crew troubles, culminating in a full-blown mutiny that he put down with characteristic forcefulness.

Brought up in Pennsylvania, Samuels left home after his father remarried. His subsequent seagoing career is covered in *From Forecastle to Cabin* but he retired after serious injury, only to forge a second successful career as the skipper of several large racing yachts in the 1870s and 1880s.

Samuels' tale details his rise from the lowest rank of his profession, a mere runaway boy, to what he sees as the acme of his own particular branch of seafaring. In Samuels' case, and in his own words: 'In her (the *Dreadnought*) I reached the top of my profession – captain of a Liverpool packet!' It has been said that any young New York boy of that time aspired to be the skipper of a Black Ball packet before President of the United States, and part of the reason Samuels wrote the book was to disabuse anyone with such aspirations of this over-romantic view. The book is important in that it provides an account which moves from the point of view of a man before the mast of no education in the early part of the text to that of the captain he eventually became, in the most prestigious post an American seaman could hold. The reader also gains a valuable insight into the daily life in perhaps the most famous of all the infamous Liverpool packets – the *Dreadnought*, a ship of almost legendary status, which has been celebrated in song, story, verse, reportage, and all manner of pictorial representation.

Samuel Samuels was born near Philadelphia, Pennsylvania, on 14 March 1825. Being 'more fond of water than school', and being unable to agree with his new stepmother and her son, he ran away aged eleven, shipping as cabin boy on a coasting vessel. He deserted and then tried to sign on various other ships and was finally signed, with another boy, George, by Captain Cozans of the schooner, *Rio*. Cozans initially reminded Samuels of a 'Sunday School teacher', but we see his early lessons in the hardships of the seagoing life: when he asked for food, he was told, 'You young rascal! I've a mind to break your jaw. The idea of a sailor saying he's hungry! Tighten your belt and take a drink of water.' There was also a rude awakening as to the uncertainties associated with marine employment, when after leaving the miserly Captain Cozans and unable to find another ship, there was no choice for him but to sign up once more with Cozans, as cook for a passenger-carrying voyage to Mobile, where Cozans joined with some pirates and wreckers in stripping an English vessel, *Emerald*. The detour proved fatal when a gale blew up and caught the *Rio* shorthanded: both boys were washed off the foot ropes by the vessel plunging and although Samuels was lucky enough to be caught by the helmsman, George was seen no more. This early trip set the pattern for the trials and dangers which Samuels tells us went hand in hand with his life at sea; he pulls no punches in the telling, and is eager not to romanticise his experiences. He writes:

> I would not commit my experiences to paper if I felt that they would in the slightest tend to induce a boy to become a sailor. The rough experience I have gone through, few could live to endure. I have seen many a man who started with me in this race of a daring and reckless life fall early on the journey, leaving his mother, wife, or sweetheart to watch and wait for one who will never return to her loving embrace, or meet her again until the sea shall be called to give up its dead.

Early in his career Samuels encountered for the first time the dreaded crimps who preyed on sailors in every port; the definition in *The Sailor's Word Book* describes them most vividly as 'Detested agents who trepan seamen, by treating, advancing money, etc, by which the dupes become indebted, and when well plied with liquor are induced to sign articles, and are shipped off, only discovering their mistake on finding themselves at sea robbed of all they possessed.'[3]

He and his companions were encouraged to desert the *Rio* at Mobile and sign on the *Jefferson*, a revenue cutter, Samuels' first experience of being 'shanghaied'. As shanghaiing is a recurring event in the first part of Samuel's career, perhaps there should be an attempt to describe both the term and the thing. *The Oxford Companion to Ships and the Sea* conjectures it to be based on an Australian aboriginal word meaning 'to catapult', ie, that seamen were 'catapulted' off to sea. The book states the term is American, but fails to make the connection between American seamen and a familiarity with Australian Aboriginal language. There is, however, a more compelling explanation grounded in the historical situation.

There was a huge growth in transatlantic emigration in the second quarter of the nineteenth century in response to the economic conditions at home in Britain, and the perceived economic possibilities to be found in America; by 1849 three hundred thousand people a year were emigrating, generating a greatly increased demand for sailors to man the emigrant ships. However, these relatively short runs from Liverpool or London to northern America were not so difficult for the recruiters as the long twenty-thousand mile voyages from Europe or America to the Far East, where voyages were measured in years, and conditions were hard. With the breaking of the monopoly held by the East India Company and the opening of Far and Near East ports to general shipping, demand for labour also increased on these runs, and recruitment was difficult. The solution was to employ agents, or gangers, to do the recruiting, and these became known as 'shanghaiers', after the port of Shanghai in China:

> . . . from 'Shanghae in China,' there were seldom any ships returning to California. To get back, therefore, they [the seamen] must make the voyage around the world . . . hence shipowners depended . . . almost exclusively on drugging the men. Crews for Shanghae were, therefore, said to be Shanghaed, and the term came into general use to represent this whole system of drugging, extortion, and cruelty.[4]

Shanghaiing would usually be centred on a brothel or tavern on the waterfront – ideally built on pilings over the river, and with a trap door that opened down into a rowing boat. It reached its apogee in the 1849 San Francisco Gold Rush, because 'gold fever was so virulent, so contagious, that as soon as a ship let go her anchor in a Californian port the whole crew deserted. Skippers, ready to sail and with no men offered premiums to any who would provide them. Human vultures answered the call and 'Frisco's waterfront became notorious for thuggery and violent kid-napping.'[5]

The system also worked to keep sailors permanently in debt to others, by signing 'advance notes' on their pay, in return for cash in hand. We see this happen to Samuels when the same crimp who initially shanghaied him reappeared offering to obtain Samuels' release from Mobile jail when the crew were imprisoned for a drunken mutiny, on condition that he signed a further advance note for another two months' wages. Samuels did so and rejoined his ship four months' wages in debt. However, on board he was taken under the wing of French Peter, a worldly wise sailor who became Samuels' mentor, beginning his thorough education in all things nautical which eventually led to his success as captain. They developed a method of smuggling and selling drink on board, which made them enough money to desert, but once again they were shanghaied onto a ship bound eventually for Liverpool. On this vessel, the *Belvedere* (Captain Oliver), Samuels experienced his first taste of the Western Ocean, that wild part of the north Atlantic Ocean that was the thoroughfare of the packet ships where his career would culminate. In this ship he met with 'Belaying Pin soup and Handspike Hash' and saw four men beaten to death by the ship's officers, the captain shrieking, 'By God I'll have my eighty dollars [money paid to the crimp] out of them or kill them.' These conditions would not have been abnormal on American ships in this era, which were renowned for their brutal treatment of crews and acquired the sobriquets 'hell ships' and 'blood boats'. Charles Domville-Fife has painted a vivid picture of the skippers and mates.

> Their hard-case skippers and bucko mates, possessed by some diabolical and inhuman blood-lust, were experts in the art of 'working up' and man-handling refractory crews; and many cases are on record of their beating a man to death with their belaying-pins and knuckle-dusters, or of subjecting him to such methods of refined cruelty that he went mad, or jumped overboard to escape from them.[6]

The crews were regarded as little better than sub-human, beaten to within an inch of their lives, and by the time Samuels reached the exalted position of captain he was to share this view, echoed in his memoirs. When the *Belvedere* reached Liverpool, it was to find that 'Of all the seaports I visited, I found none so filthy and degrading. Drunkenness was almost universal. The saloons were only shut at midnight; and on Sundays during church hours. When God's temple on earth was closed, the devil opened his palace gates.'

Further adventures included a close encounter with pirates in the Caribbean Sea, when French Peter's insider knowledge of the way that pirates worked contributed to their narrow escape, and Samuels even spent a short time on a Texas navy frigate, at a time when Texas was an independent republic, and Galveston a shanty town populated by 'outlaws of all nations'. With French Peter no longer by his side, the teenaged Samuels found another old salt in the form of Jack, a Guernseyman, to continue his education. 'My idea is to make a sailor of you,' Jack told the teenager, 'I shall be a happy man when I see you tread the quarterdeck.' However, Jack did not live to see his protégé move up in the world, falling casualty to a storm at sea, but Samuels identifies this as the point when he took to his books and began to make a serious study of navigation in his mid teens. He demonstrates to us that his success in life was due to his application and determination, but these two experienced seaman-mentors set him along his way, and taught him much in the way of practical, hands-on seamanship in his early career, which contributed much to his later skill as captain of the 'wild boat of the Atlantic'.

Samuels married young and became a father, which he saw as a steadying influence on his life, and the end of his unruly sailor habits, and began to travel purposefully from ship to ship, gaining experience along the way. Eventually he achieved the rank of mate, and then, through a resignation at Amsterdam, suddenly became a captain at twenty-one. He made a trip through the Greek Isles and the Bosporus, was offered and declined the Admiralship of the Turkish Navy,

helped a woman escape from a harem at Constantinople, then returned to Rotterdam where, his voyage
being judged a success, he was told he might take his
family with him next trip. This was to Leghorn and
Batavia, the ship's owner 'not forgetting to mention that
he had not insured the ship – knowing my having my
family on board would be sufficient insurance for him.'

His adventures continued apace. Rescued from an
explosive situation at Pisa by a detachment of American
naval officers arriving in the nick of time from Leghorn,
Samuels then put to sea for Batavia with eighty
thousand dollars in old Spanish silver. The piratical
fishermen of whom he had fallen foul followed him at
their peril: Samuels' 'Christian spirit forsook' him such
that he opened fire at his pursuers, and 'how many were
killed or hurt [he] never knew.' In these episodes
Samuels demonstrates the qualities of self-reliance and
resourcefulness he sees as essential to his success as a
captain; he tells us that 'A shipmaster is called upon to
act many parts in the drama of life: sailor, sailmaker,
rigger, carpenter, painter, and, in fact, cook, doctor,
lawyer, clergyman, navigator, merchant, and banker',
and the reader cannot fail to be impressed by the
indomitable courage of a man who could not only
engineer a replacement rudder, but was prepared to
operate on his own leg as well. We see his self-asserted
leadership qualities once more when taking passage on
a Dutch steamer and caught in a storm, Samuels was

called upon to assume command. He brought the ship safe to shore and was 'made quite a lion', but his future did not lie in Holland.

Rather than remain in Europe, whatever employment was offered, he returned to America where his dream became a reality and he was offered the command of the Liverpool packet, *Dreadnought*, in 1853 – especially built for him he tells us, a ship that eventually garnered to itself more gossip, fame and infamy than the rest of all the packets put together:

> There is a CRACK packet – A packet of FAME –
> She's out of New York, and the DREADNOUGHT'S her name
> And bound for those seas where the great winds do blow
> She's the Liverpool Packet – O Lord let her go.
> *Foc'sle shanty*

A 'packet' was an early name for a piece of shipping mail – private letters, contracts, documents being sent to and from embassies, colonies and outposts – and the word became associated with the ships that carried them as early as the sixteenth century. Throughout the wars of the eighteenth century these craft, often only lightly armed, relied upon speed for their security. The packet ship – or packet liner or simply, packet – to which Samuels was appointed captain was a very different vessel. They sailed mainly between American and British ports and, significantly, operated to a schedule, and it was the attempt to maintain such a regular service over the wilds of the North Atlantic that placed such daunting demands on ships and men.

After the end of the Second American War (1812–1814) with trade and emigration beginning to increase between America and Britain, a stabilised and guaranteed service between the two countries became essential. As with anything where money is concerned, reliability was paramount. The Black Ball Line was the first to introduce such a service in 1818, and the ships carried freight and passengers as well as mail. The vessels were easily distinguished by the black ball sewn or painted onto the fore-topsail, and perhaps needed to be for there was soon strong competition. The Red Cross Line, under the flag of which the *Dreadnought* sailed, and the Swallowtail Line were just two of many companies that were established to exploit the Atlantic packet trade. And this American enterprise led to American domination; British merchantmen surrendered and sought their trade elsewhere, particularly in the Far East and other outposts of empire.

Samuels was to become perhaps the most famous of the packet captains and his vessel, the *Dreadnought*, a legend. She was designed and built by Currier & Townsend at Newbury Port, Massachusetts, and launched in 1853. She was what has come to be termed a 'medium' clipper, a three-masted ship of 212 feet overall and 1,414 tons, built along clipper lines, but smaller and stouter than the later and more glamorous clippers like the *Lightning* or *Sovereign of the Seas*. Designed to be worked in the rough conditions of the Western Ocean, the bows were fuller and the gear heavier, and while she was fast, she was not as fast as the later extreme clippers. As Samuels wrote of *Dreadnought* himself, 'she possessed the merit of being able to bear driving as long as her sails and spars would stand.' He was to make any number of remarkable passages.

She sailed on her maiden voyage on 6 December 1853, bound for Liverpool carrying a cargo of corn, cotton, potash, bacon and staves, and was to make the round trip back to New York in fifty-eight days, and earn her owners a handsome profit of $40,000. On the returning westward trip, the main income was generated by carrying emigrants. Between 1815 and 1854 more than four million emigrants left British ports and the conditions they encountered on the packet ships were grim. Provision for privacy and sanitation was minimal and, in the early years, starvation and disease were rampant. This passage, against the prevailing westerlies, could take between thirteen and sixty days. Once, in January 1863 when six days out of Liverpool, *Dreadnought*, encountering a severe gale, broke her rudder and was forced to make for Fayal where she spent fifty-two days undergoing repairs. Most of her runs, however, were spectacularly fast and she is credited with the shortest passages between the two ports. It is no wonder that she was nicknamed 'the wild boat of the Atlantic'.

Samuels left the *Dreadnought* in 1863 and she was never to repeat the outstanding passages achieved under his tough command. In July 1869 she drifted ashore at Cape Penas, off Tierra del Fuego, and was wrecked, her crew spending seventeen days in two lifeboats before being picked up.

The Liverpool packets became notorious for their 'hard-driving' and for their captains, officers and crew – all of whom sought to outdo each other in bravado and brutality: 'Men to whom fists and the knuckle-duster took precedence over the sextant'.[7] The crews, mainly Liverpool-Irish, became known as packet rats, and many refused to sail in any other type of vessel – as none other offered the same amounts of unending work in appalling conditions, drink, and the excitement they craved. As a general rule Yankee sailors avoided the cold seas of the Western Ocean, preferring the sunnier climes of the Pacific; packet skippers had to make do with what they could find and the Liverpool packet rat – tough, drunken and irascible – evolved to meet the brutal conditions found in the packet ships. Here is an American sailor's description of packet rats leaving New Orleans:

At dark the circus began in earnest. The cuss word and the crunch of the belaying pin were continually in our ears and on our heads. Every little while one of the mates would be overpowered and go down under a yelling and kicking crowd; but only for a moment when the others would come to his rescue; and, as they were sober, it was easy to pull off the sailors and club and kick then out of the way . . . How long I slept I have not the slightest idea, but was rudely awakened by being dragged out of my bunk by the hair of the head. It was the mate who had come across my combing again and amid a volley of curses he kicked, thumped and flung me out of the door on deck. He picked me up by the hair again, and standing me against the rail, grasped me by the throat, and, with my head jambed solidly against a dead-eye, hit me hard as he could right on my eye, laying my cheek open to the bone and giving me a mark I shall carry to my grave. Believing my life in danger, I tried to get out my knife, but my arms were jambed in such a way I could not reach it; and just as I was scringing up my face for a second blow I felt his grasp on my throat release, and he fell away to a wild Irish yell.

'Ho, ye blackguard, I have you now! Ye murderin' brute, ye!' and all the time good, solid blows were being rained down on the mate, who was on his knees and the deck, trying to rise, cursing for McDonald and Parker (the other officers).

The blood was pouring down my face in a perfect

torrent, and I felt weak and dizzy, but I got a good kick on his jaw, and another in his ribs, besides a couple of punches which, though weak, I found highly gratifying. All the time the Irishman was working away like a pile-driver with something I couldn't see what, and yelling and cursing like a madman; and the mate, who must have had a head of iron to stand the terrific blows he was getting, now began to shout he was being murdered.

As I was shifting round to get in another kick, somebody caught me by the neck and threw me down on my back, and a heavy boot was placed on my chest, while I heard a strange voice say, 'Let up, there! Or I'll blow your damned head off!'

'Who the hell are you?' said the Irishman, who had just been grabbed round the waist by one of the mates.

'I'm captain of this ship, and this thing's gone far enough!'[8]

The last two anecdotes from Samuels' book tell of the mutiny on the *Dreadnought* by the Liverpool Bloody Forties, one of the most notorious gangs of sailors, which lasted from the Mersey almost to New York, but these hardened characters apparently met their match in this particular captain; his indomitable will and muscular Christianity ensured their defeat and he tells us that they left his ship reformed men. In case the reader still doubts Samuels' strength of character and toughness, the story of his broken leg should convince;

suffering a compound fracture of the leg, he set it himself, with a saw lying handy should he himself have to amputate, 'as no one else would. I gave instructions for the taking up of the arteries, in case I became too weak. But felt it was better to die in making the attempt than to die without making it.' And so this rollicking tale draws to a close as, aged thirty-eight and after his accident, Samuels relinquishes command of the *Dreadnought*, and ends his autobiography.

After the *Dreadnought*, Samuels captained the steamer *John Rice*, then he became general superintendent of the quartermaster's department in New York city, seeing to repairs, stores, and sailing schedules. In 1865 he commanded the *McClellan* at the taking of Fort Fisher. He captained the steamer *Fulton*, and spent some years racing yachts. In 1872 he organised the Samana Bay Company of Santo Domingo, with some sort of understanding that the US Government should acquire a part of the bay as a naval station, but in 1874 was expelled by the new Dominican government. In 1876 he ran the Rousseau Electric Signal Company, and in 1878 became general superintendent of the Pacific Mail Steamship Company, San Francisco, following which in 1881 he led the United States Steam Heating and Power Company in New York.

The present volume, *From the Forecastle to the Cabin* was published in 1877. The book contains nothing of his life after the *Dreadnought*. As stated at the beginning of this introduction, in captaining the *Dreadnought*, Samuels considered himself to have reached 'the top of my profession'.

In the course of the book Samuels is at great pains to say that not one in a thousand could have borne what he had borne – and lived to tell the tale, and that the book had been written to deter boys from going to sea. This, of course, is not so – no one knew better than Samuels how much the world depends on sea commerce, especially to a still emerging nation as America was at that time. He comments that no one knows more about human nature, or is more honest in his own way, than the merchant seaman: 'An education that fits him for anything except Wall Street – for, while no class of men understands human nature better than the sailor, none are as easily swindled.'

1. I begin my seafaring life. Down the Schuylkill I port the helm in an emergency. Falsely charged with snoring. A cruel remedy for seasickness. My nerves unstrung by tales of river pirates I desert for the first time.

AT THE AGE of eleven I took leave of home. My father having remarried, my stepmother and her son and I soon began having such differences that a house the size of the Capitol could not hold us. As her son would not run away to promote the harmony of the family, in 1836 at the age of eleven I ran away myself.

Being more fond of water than school, and having devoured the works of Cooper and Marryat, I determined on a sea life. After one or two minor trips, I found myself as cook and cabin boy on the schooner *Hampton Westcott* (Captain Blew), carrying coal down the Schuylkill for New York. Claiming I knew how to steer, I was sent to the helm, as I was too light to be of much service hoisting sail.

Nearing Grey's Ferry Bridge, drawn to let us pass, the

captain yelled to me, 'Port, you villain, or you'll have the masts out of her!'

This order confused me, as I did not know the word 'port' was equivalent to 'larboard', which I was used to hearing. Fortunately, the idea struck me that Philadelphia was a port, so I pushed the tiller that way. But we would still have been dismasted had not the captain's wife rushed up out of the cabin and let go the main peak halyards, thereby saving the mainsail. During all this, not knowing what would become of me, I was about to jump overboard when the mate's wife seized me by the back of the neck, saying, 'Don't be frightened. The captain's my brother and very kind to boys.'

This did not reassure me, especially when I saw the captain now coming aft with fire in his eyes and a piece of ratline in his hand. But his wife interposed, 'Don't you dare touch that boy! You spoke to him like a brute, frightening the life out of him.'

Seeing who the real captain and mate were, I made myself very agreeable to the ladies by telling them pitiful stories of the home life of 'Jack Williams'; I had, naturally, like many sailors, gone aboard under an assumed name.

Although that day had been the most trying of my short life, sleep was a stranger that night. All hands lived and slept in the cabin: the captain, mate, three men, and the two females. These latter immediately began questioning me.

'Now, sonny,' said one, 'Tell us who are you, and where you really came from?'

'That cock-and-bull story about your poor widowed mother,' said the other, 'With the seven little children. We know you are a runaway.'

They then began to question me so vigorously that twice the captain mildly called, 'Mary! Do let the boy alone, and turn in.'

After a second invitation, she replied, 'Shut up, or I will throw a boot at you.'

The mate, seeing there would be no sleep unless matters were resolved, now yelled at me, 'You young pup! Tell what you know or I'll lick you within an inch of your life!'

Knowing that these were Jersey people, looked on in those days as sort of half-savage Spaniards, I answered all the ladies' questions until they exhausted themselves, after which I was allowed to sleep, only to be punched by my bunkmate, Horace, who said if I did not stop snoring he would smother me.

I soon fell off again, only to get a second thump which I thought had broken all my ribs. I cried out that it was not I that snored, and this was seconded by the shrill voice of the mate's wife, who said it was Horace himself as she 'knew the sound of his bugle'. All quieted down until Horace began to toot again. As the noise reached the intensity of a foghorn, I slipped out of bed, and lay down on the locker on the opposite side of the cabin. The mate now got out of bed, took up the pitcher of water, and dashed it into Horace's face. Horace jumped up, the two men clinched, then all hands joined in.

As it was now three in the morning and day was beginning to break, the schooner got under way. I was told to straighten up the cabin. As I was making my toilet, the captain's wife, observing I had no comb, presented me with one. At that age I had a very heavy mass of black, curly hair where now only one solitary spear is left upstanding like a spar buoy in slack water.

We worked down the Delaware, anchoring in the breakwater overnight. At daylight, the wind hauled to the southwest, and we shaped our course, wing and wing, for New York. I had never been in open sea before. The motion of the vessel unsteadied me, and instead of entering the door I bumped against the side of the galley in which my duties lay. I became careless of what I did, filling the freshwater kettle with saltwater and, of course, spoiling the coffee and mush.

I have never yet met the writer who could describe the absolute misery of seasickness. Those who have endured the horrors of *mal-de-mer* will sympathise when they hear I was never free from this plague during my first three years at sea. That particular June morning, I threw myself on the fore hatch, utterly reckless of everything, even though there was a sea on, and water swashed over both the decks and myself. I made a resolve that if I ever got to shore, the canals should be sea enough thereafter; that I should drive one of those towpath rafts in which, when shortening sail, the captain or his wife simply cries 'Whoa!' to the horse. One of the sailors now offered to effect a cure. He went to the harness cask, took out a small bit of raw pork, to which he tied a piece of rope yarn, and told me to hold on to the end of the yarn and swallow the pork, and then pull it up – two or three times! I would have swallowed a handspike had I been told it would alleviate my sufferings. Down went the pork. I did not realise what I had done till I tried to pull it up, when a fright seized me. Holding the rope yarn with both hands, I ran aft to find Captain Blew, encountering Deborah, the mate's wife. She quieted me as the captain took hold of the yarn and yanked the pork up. She was beside herself. Seizing a belaying pin, and being a muscular woman, she used it with all the skill of a Liverpool packet mate on the funny man who had played his practical joke.

Abreast of the Tavern Houses (now Long Brand) the wind hauled to the west and the sea became smooth. I began to notice things, and now the ladies decided to 'rig me out' in some of the captain's old clothes. The trousers would have fitted had I been allowed to use the side pockets as armholes, but they put suspenders on me, cutting the trousers off below the knee, in spite of which they still touched the deck. But I felt the mantles of all the great navigators now fall on me, and I would make a mark in history.

The wind lasted just enough to allow us to work around Sandy Hook and anchor in the Horseshoe. Anchor watches were set, with strict orders to look out for pirates. This word aroused a lively interest in me, and I listened with bated breath to the crew's many stories of these robbers and murderers: stories, for my benefit, not drawn mildly. The captain's wife, Mrs Blew, noticing my frightened look, suggested that the yarns be cut short, and that all hands turn in. That night there was little need for any watch than myself, for I doubt if I closed my eyes.

The following morning we worked up to New York. While we were passing Gibbet Island it was pointed out to me as the place where those selfsame pirates were hanged. We made fast at the foot of Rector Street and began to discharge cargo. Pirates again were the topic during supper when two or three of the captain's friends came on board. They related experience of robberies, beatings, gaggings, dismastings and everything movable, including the ship's boy, being stolen and rowed off. I was dreadfully frightened, and fell into an uneasy sleep that night.

Suddenly I awakened with the cabin in pitchy darkness, the only sound the ticking of the watch hanging on the forward bulkhead. I heard someone jump from the wharf to the rail; then footsteps coming aft; then the companion slide being pushed back. Step by step someone came down into the cabin, but I was too terror-stricken to cry out. I listened as the footsteps passed me, heard the watch taken from the hook and its ticking cease as if put into someone's pocket.

Then, the steps seeming to come towards my berth, I gave a terrific yell of 'Murder! Murder! Man in the hold! Man in the hold!'

The women joined in as a chorus, and the men began grappling one another, the uproar being increased by the voices of the women shouting to their husbands, 'Are you alive? Are you alive!'

All yelled to me to get a light, as I had the tinderbox in bed with me to keep it dry. I lit a candle, then got down behind a table holding the candle over my head, which I kept below the table. The uproar ceased on the discovery that no one had pushed back the slide, come into the cabin, or removed the watch. All hands were scratched and bruised, and I would have received a severe whipping had it not been for the women, who, however, were angry with me for causing such a disturbance. It was half-past one. The mate got out the whisky bottle, and after all hands had a few drops, several times over, good nature was restored, and all turned in. I was told I could let the light burn if I was afraid.

Unable to sleep, I kept my eyes fixed upon the companionway. It began to rain, large drops pattering on the deck with such force I feared it would be stove in; I had never heard anything like it before. And now the slide *was* being pushed back, and the legs of a man appeared. Presently I saw a begrimed face.

He asked in a low voice, 'May I come down?' at the same time descending softly.

I was not frightened as the light was burning, but called, 'Captain! There is a man in the cabin!' He replied he would 'whale the hide' off me. This re-awakened everybody, when the stranger repeated his request. After some palaver, he was allowed to sit on the floor until daylight. At dawn, the mate told him to go ashore, or he would boot him. I was ordered to make the galley fire, but refused unless someone would accompany me, afraid a thief might be there waiting to murder me.

In three days the vessel was discharged, ready to return. I had made up my mind that she would leave without me, and ran away that afternoon. I had nothing but what I stood in, and not a cent in my pocket. That night I slept in a butcher's cart near Franklin Market.

2. I sign on the schooner *Rio* (Captain Cozans) who does not believe in food. I steer the ship myself while the captain lies drunk. I steal a pig and make two dollars. Unable to find a vessel I sign again with Cozans as cook. He takes me home for his sister, Sara, to teach me the culinary arts. I fall in love with her. We sail for Mobile. Through the captain's greed we are almost wrecked in a great storm. I lose my friend overboard.

BEFORE MORNING I was disturbed by a brutal driver, who, coming to hitch up his horse, gave me a heavy kick. The yell I gave caused a crowd, which so angered him that he threw me to the pavement. My head struck the stones, and I must have passed out. When brought to by some kind-hearted market women, I learned that a general fight had taken place on my account, which ended by the watchman arresting the combatants. I had an ugly scalp wound and was badly bruised, but no bones broken.

After receiving a cup of coffee and a chunk of bread and butter, I felt myself a hero, and fairly launched in life. I sauntered along the docks to find a berth. Some skippers found me too small. Others called me a young blackguard, and told me to go home and bring my mother, adding that if she proved good-looking perhaps they would take me.

I finally boarded the schooner *Rio* (Captain Cozans) lying at a pier near Wall Street.

He said at once, 'All right, my young tar, go home and bring your clothes. I will wait half an hour as the flood tide is making, so hurry back.' I replied that as I lived too far, and my clothes did not amount to much, I would leave them for my brothers and join as I was.

'I like the way you speak,' he said, 'and will be a father to you. Can you steer?'

'Yes, sir.'

'Cook?'

'Yes, sir.'

'Been at sea before?'

'Not much.'

He spoke so kindly, he reminded me of a Sunday-school teacher. But, oh dear! I later found the lambskin covered a wolf. He had engaged another boy named George, from Providence, and we two completed the crew. We were bound to Newport, RI. As George and I were too light to hoist sail, two Negro wharf-rats were hired for five cents each to help us set canvas, and cast off our lines. We ran up the East River. The captain, finding I could steer better than George, kept me at the tiller all day. I felt very important until the novelty wore off, and my stomach became a vacuum. At three in the afternoon, I gently hinted to Captain Cozans that if George would take the tiller I would cook the dinner.

'No dinner,' I was told. 'If you're hungry, go down the cabin where there's some bread and cheese.'

George and I went below and finished the remains of what had been a pound of cheese and some biscuits. The captain evidently did not believe in variety, nor in laying in stores to be wasted. He had bought the schooner cheap in New York, with money earned by close economy: his first command. He expected to run up to Newport in twenty hours, and therefore had no reason to provide food. Now the wind changed, gaining strength as night advanced. At 8pm we furled the flying jib, after taking in the main gaff topsail. The watches were now set, the captain and George having the first below. My orders were, just after we tacked close under the Connecticut shore, to let her stand on until close under Long Island, then tack again to the northward. I was to call the watch at midnight, earlier if it blew any harder. Prior to this he had been below many times to look at the glass. But from the smell in the cabin I judged that the glass he inspected did not contain mercury, more likely 'Jersey lightning'.[9] But in this I must have been mistaken, as it was generally given out that he was a prohibitionist.

Here was I, a lad of twelve, in command of the deck. Lord Nelson could not have felt greater responsibility. I became very tired, but the freshening wind prevented me from falling asleep. The land suddenly loomed up high and I thought it time to tack, fearing I had stood in too close. I put the tiller into the becket, and ran forward, making fast the jib draw rope. I put the helm down to let her come around. Becketing the tiller again, I went forward and let the jib draw once around. Now, with the land astern, I felt safe, and judged it time to call the captain. Looking down the cabin I found the light out, and therefore could not tell the time. I left it until midway across the Sound, and ventured down again. His loud snoring scared me and I feared to wake him. George I could not find, nor could I stay down because of what might be happening on deck.

We continued towards Connecticut, the wind still increasing. In tacking again, the shaking of the sails was so violent, the captain awakened himself. Jumping up, he found the schooner staggering along, her rail under water. His language to me was anything but classical. George now steered while the captain and I went forward to check the ground tackle for anchoring. I was terribly tired and hungry. I asked the captain if there was anything more to eat.

'Do you think I keep a hotel?' was his reply. 'I did

not ship you to be stuffed like a turkey with truffles. Aren't salt beef and pork good enough for you?'

'Where are they?' I asked.

'You young rascal! I've a mind to break your jaw. The idea of a sailor saying he's hungry! Why, I've been a week without food. Tighten your belt and take a drink of water.'

I went below. A scent led me to the captain's berth where, under his pillow, I found his bottle. After that, I cared no more for hunger than I did for his breaking my jaw. I turned in all standing, and in a moment my dreams carried me back to my mother: her last dying look on me, her hands clasped as though praying for me. I was too young to understand, few children do, what it is to lose a mother. In my dream she had brought me home such a package of candy, and was caressing and fondling me. This caressing was now the hand of the captain hauling me out of my berth.

'Why did you not turn out when called?' he asked with an oath.

When I got on deck, still dazed, day was breaking. I found the schooner heading for a bay – perhaps Glen Cove. Once anchored, the captain gave me two dollars, and sent me and George ashore to forage provisions. As there were no stores, I went to the nearest farmhouse, about a quarter of a mile from the beach. I arranged a pitiful story as I approached the farmer's wife feeding her chickens.

I had scarcely begun my narrative of hunger and hardship, when she said: 'You young liar! I lost three dozen of my finest chickens last week to a fellow looking just like you – *his* tale was a *shipwreck*! Now leave pretty quick or I'll call the men out of the fields and set the dog on you!'

I saw nothing would prevail, so we turned and started for the boat. On the way we passed through an apple orchard, but I knew she was still staring after us. When a short distance from the boat I turned to find myself hidden by trees in the orchard. Nearby was a sow, with a litter of good-sized sucklings. I called to George to shove off the boat, while I seized one of the young porkers by the snout to prevent it squealing. Holding it before me, I jumped into the boat, tied its feet, and gagged it with my handkerchief.

When we came alongside, Captain Cozans, with an oath, gave vent to his disappointment at not getting some bread, and uttered a stronger one when I told him I had paid four dollars for a pig. I told him the old woman was going to bake that afternoon, and would send us a loaf. It did not take long to make a fire and boil the pig, there being no convenience for roasting. There was no salt or dressing, but hunger is a good sauce and there was little left when we finished. Hunger also sharpens the wits – but is an enemy to honesty.

In the afternoon we got under way, and next morning arrived at Newport. Here I left the vessel. The captain refused to pay me the two dollars which I said I had paid extra for the pig, but gave me fifty cents, declaring it my due for three days' work. I suppose it was, and felt myself rich with it, and the captain's two dollars that I already had. I went ashore happy, bought a shirt and pair of shoes and looked around for another vessel. But there was nothing here except fishing smacks.

I fared pretty hard for three or four days, then again met Captain Cozans who asked if I would like to ship to Mobile with him as cook as he was taking passengers. I agreed, and we went to his house where he said his sister, Sara, would give me culinary instruction. He said she was an adept at shortcake and cornbread, knew how to fry fish and ham, and at baking beans had no superior. Sara was also very clever with the needle, and reefed in some of her brother's clothes to fit me. A nice girl, but ugly! Pockmarked, snub-nosed, redheaded – all the boys avoided her. I fell in love with her, however, because she was so good to me. I believe I whipped every boy in town to whom she owed a grudge, and was sorry when the time came to leave her.

Our cargo for Mobile was lumber, potatoes, cabbages, onions, pigs and chickens. We had three cabin passengers, who, with the captain, owned the cargo. All thought they were sailing south to make a fortune. The crew consisted of the captain, the mate (Ball, a Block Islander), two sailors, George and myself. We set sail. The cabin on the *Rio* was very small. There were two lengths of berths on each side. Two of the passengers slept on the transom. Stern windows gave light from aft when the weather was fine. A skylight lighted the cabin from above. Our provisions were limited; while everyone seemed to have access to my storeroom, and a right to help himself.

As to the cooking, for the first day or two this duty devolved upon one of the men, I was so dreadfully seasick, but after a few quarts of warm saltwater I soon became my old self. We had run down to the Bahama Bank when the main gaff topsail chafed off, and orders were given to lower the mainsail and reeve the sheet again. I immediately offered to reeve it without having the sail lowered, and started up the mast by the hoops. The rolling of the schooner slatted the mainsail so that the gaff jerked very hard and when I undertook to shin it, the captain yelled, 'Come down! Now!'

But as all were looking at me, I had to show how smart I was. Just as I had pointed the sheet through the block, the mainsail gave a heavy flap and I was overboard. All on board was confusion while I swam around leisurely waiting for a boat to be lowered; stunned, but enjoying all the fuss I had created. A threatened 'rope's ending' from the captain was nothing to the great man I now felt myself.

At 6pm I was sitting on my chopping-block at the galley door, again thinking of my illustrious future, when the mate put his head out of the cabin scuttle and called me aft. I found the captain stirring his tea and looking very grave. A froth like that of new ale was at least an inch above the cup.

'Cook,' said he, 'What's this?'

'Tea, sir.'

'Taste it.' I did. It tasted very strongly of soap.

'And?' he now enquired.

'Tea, sir.'

'Drink it!' I did.

'And?'

'Tea, sir.'

'You young liar. Get forward! You beat Tom Pepper!' Later I learned Tom Pepper was a sailor kicked out of hell for lying. I realised that a piece of soap, to which someone had helped himself out of my locker, must have fallen into the sugar barrel, and thence into the captain's teacup.

We crossed the Gulf Stream and ran along the Florida reefs. We stopped at Key West where we sold some of our cargo, and I bought some coral and shells to take home – should I ever see home again.

We weighed for Mobile, and west of that port discovered the English bark, *Emerald*, ashore and several small vessels nearby. These latter were wreckers – pirates, I should say, from the way they were stripping the ship. In such a business our captain and crew were not above taking a hand, I being left on board with the passengers.

Night approached, and with it a gale called a 'Norther'. Our people were too busy on the wreck to notice and when the first blast struck we started our anchor, and before we fetched up we had dragged nearly a mile. With much difficulty we got our crew back on board. It now blew so hard we had no supper cooked that night as the weather was too bad and, as far as I was concerned, I hoped it would continue. At 8pm I turned in. At midnight I was called to shorten sail. George and I went out to stow the jib while the rest were reefing, when the vessel made a heavy plunge, washing George and me off the foot ropes. I was caught by the man at the tiller but poor George was seen no more.

We hove to, and all hands went below. Presently a heavy sea struck and swept the decks. During the next lull we furled the foresail and hove to under a main trysail. My galley was washed overboard, worrying everyone but myself. No more cooking for me! That night I slept as happy as a monkey in a menagerie. From then on, we lived on raw ham, salt herring, and onions.

The next day and night the storm continued in violence, without a break. The third night, about 11pm the captain shook me, saying, 'Boy! Wake up! Turn out! Say your prayers!'

The scene in the cabin was dismal: the water was knee-deep, the passengers huddled on the transom. I tried to pick up the captain's chart which was floating around, but the captain said, 'There's no more use for that,' adding, 'as we're all drowned before daylight.'

At the same time I heard the leadsman giving the draft, which was rapidly shoaling. Though none knew where we were, it was decided at six fathoms to run up the centreboard and try to beach her. A heavy roll warned us there was no time to be lost. The next instant she raised her stern high in the air, and with a fearful crash as the sea rolled from under her, she struck. Out went the cabin lights. The next breaker stove in her stern ports. The *Rio* again mounted the sea, was carried forward with fearful velocity, and again struck. The cabin filled, and we were all engaged in a death struggle to get on deck. Two were drowned. When we recovered, we found that we had been carried over a bar, and were in four fathoms of perfectly smooth water. The vessel was half-swamped and no land was visible. The flashes of lightning, and the roaring of the wind and sea made me grow ten years older in the same number of minutes. The horrible shrieks during the struggle in the cabin ring in my ears even now. This was the memorable hurricane in the Gulf in 1836.

All hands began pumping as the wind gradually abated and the long wished for day broke. Still no land could be seen. By 4pm the water was out of the hold and the captain gave each of us a good stiff glass of rum. The night came out starlight, followed by a gorgeous sunrise. We saw islands all around and nearby the dry sandbar over which the sea had carried us. We did not know where we were until late in the afternoon, when a wrecking sloop came along and offered to pilot us. The wrecker would not reveal our position until our captain had struck a bargain. Then we found that we were off the Mississippi, and had been driven over a bar which extended from the Grand Grozier to the Bretain Island.

We set our tattered sails again for Mobile. As we passed by where the *Emerald* had lain there was nothing to be seen but a few timbers. Our captain hurled an anathema at her, and wished she had gone to Davy Jones before he had ever seen her. But our loss of life, and the profits of the voyage, can only be charged to his greed and want of honesty.

3. I desert and join the revenue brig, *Jefferson*. Aged twelve I am ordered a dozen lashes. My first 'sea chum' French Peter. Taken back aboard the *Rio* then jailed. Restored to the *Jefferson* Peter begins my instruction. Smuggling liquor we make money to desert. We are shanghaied for Liverpool.

AT MOBILE WE were greeted by the usual crimps, who told us that we had arrived in 'high-water times', that the pay by the run to Liverpool was eighty dollars, to Havre ninety! But the best chance, and one by which we could get away that night, was to ship on the revenue brig, *Jefferson*, paying eighteen dollars a month. Two of our crewmen and myself decided we would sign. How lucky, we thought. Eighteen dollars a month, and nothing but sail around the bay and live on the fat of the land, with two glasses of grog a day, and plum duff twice a week. When grog and duff are offered, Jack yields at once and follows his leader, as the camel follows the music of his driver.

That night, when all were asleep in the cabin of the *Rio*, the two men and I slipped on deck, where we were met by the crimps, who took charge of our baggage and led us to the grog shop, the watchman lending a hand, though the law prohibited any one carrying bundles through the streets after 9pm. The watchmen of those days were quite up to those of the present.

The crimps told me I would ship as an AB[10] – but that my only duties would be steering the captain's gig, of which I would be coxswain, seeing no one squirted tobacco juice around the cabin door and, above all, to see that there were no quids spat out around the main fife rail as they stained the paint. I felt equal to perform these duties with any man and signed for six months, and for two months' advance pay – thirty-six dollars. This money was immediately taken by the crimps and for it I was rigged in a man-of-war suit of duck, and a straw hat, the whole maybe worth five dollars.

When I remonstrated with the people involved the watchman told me if I did not shut up he would take me to the calaboose, while the old woman that kept the crimp's house said she had cashed an order on me that afternoon, and that if only she were a man she would give me a licking for robbing an innocent widow. My shipmates, who had complained more vociferously, had apparently already been drugged and gagged before taken on board the *Jefferson*. When I was delivered by the crimps to the officer of the deck and the boatswain,

the officer, seeing my troubled face, asked the reason.
The crimps told him that after receiving my advance I
had tried to run away. When I tried to speak, the boatswain promised me a dozen lashes if I said another word.

At 4am all hands were piped to raise the anchor. We
got under way, proceeded down the bay about twelve
miles, then anchored. The crew consisted of Captain
Foster, who was not on board; First Lieutenant
McLane, of Scotch descent, who was constantly
grinding his teeth, and a great believer in the cat-of-
nine-tails; Second Lieutenant Sampson, a large,
good-natured man from Maine; Third Lieutenant
Smoot from Virginia, a sharp, thin-faced fellow who did
not know much; the usual number of petty officers; and
sixty men forward. The *Jefferson*, with her four broadside carronades and Long-Tom swivel was supposed to
be a match for any pirates or smugglers infesting the
Gulf of Mexico.

After the decks were holystoned[11], and brasswork
and guns polished, all hands were piped to breakfast.
Everything was new to me. I was like a cat drinking her
early morning milk, I enjoyed it so much. After
breakfast, stations were piped. I, the smallest, was
appointed fore royal yard man. Now we were piped
aloft to mend sails; that is, to loose and refurl sails. The
piping was perfect Greek to me, but I watched the rest
of the crew, and tried to do as they did. As I had never
furled a square sail, I rolled it up as best I could while

the boatswain piped continually at me, and all hands on their yards – their own sails furled – stared at me. When Lieutenant McLane could stand it no longer he shook his fist at me in such a way I felt keelhauling at least would be my punishment. A Boston boy named Nickerson was sent up to show me how to furl a royal.

He did this very kindly, but sadly, saying, 'How you will catch it back on deck! I have seen four dozen served out for much less. But it will only be a few strips of flesh torn off your back, which will give you something to brag about when a man – taking a couple of dozen and not winking. The sailors will feel proud of you, too, if you take it quietly. While it will send McLane mad if you show you don't give a damn for him or his boatswain's cats.'

On deck, all hands were called to witness punishment. I was seized up by the thumbs to the main fife rail, my body bent forward, and my back bared ready for the lashes. One dozen was to be my punishment. I did not utter a word as I was determined, Indian-like, to die rather than ask for mercy. But now a loud murmur of dissatisfaction was heard among the crew at my treatment and the boatswain, ready to strike, hesitated. Mr Sampson hurriedly approached McLane. Words passed in an undertone; and I was ordered to be cut down. McLane asked me how I dared ship as an AB.

When I told him the circumstances, and what I had been told my duties were to be, all hands gave vent to loud laughter, whereas but a few moments before they were ready to mutiny and risk being shot rather than see me flogged. I was never sure if Mr Sampson had saved me because of the serious consequences he saw threatening but, speaking kindly to me, he told me to go forward. My feelings gave vent in tears as I thanked him. I later learned that French Peter, the desperado of the forecastle, had initially offered to take my punishment and undoubtedly would have led the mutiny.

Flogging had been a pastime on this vessel, and the crew had determined to put an end to it. My case gave them their chance. After this, Peter claimed me as his own. He said that I had good stuff in me, perhaps even the makings of a boatswain. This man played a very prominent part in shaping my future and I shall speak of him again.

For the three succeeding days, we constantly exercised handling sails, working guns, etc. On the third day a schooner, with a sheriff and posse and several captains, including Captain Cozans, came alongside. All hands were mustered, and each captain picked out his men and took them away, the *Jefferson* losing about half her crew. We had all had our two months' advance from the government and this easy submission to the civil authorities eventually cost Lieutenant McLane his place.

We were taken ashore before a magistrate, where the captains told their stories. Mine, Cozans, said that his two men and I had shipped at Newport for the round voyage, and then deserted. I tried to tell the magistrate that I had not signed any articles, but was told to hush up. When I attempted to speak again, I was grabbed by the throat, violently hustled out of the court, and locked up with the rest of the men from the *Jefferson*. Presently, some lawyers like the shysters who frequent the 'Tombs' in New York City, came and offered to get us out for ten dollars each.

As I had not the wherewithal, I was left in jail. The food was bad, the company the scourings of a vile city: murderers, burglars, pickpockets. With these companions I spent nineteen days observing humanity in all its degraded forms. The lesson taught me was that liberty and honesty are synonymous. I determined never to be in prison again. The men passed the time in card-playing, boxing, wrestling, dancing. One thing I did learn well was boxing, taught me by a Jim Sweeney, whom I later met under other circumstances. I also did laundry work. One morning I would wash my shirt, and go without until it was dry; the next day I would give my ducks a swim, presenting the appearance of a young Highlander. My wardrobe, it will be understood, was what was known as an 'Irish fit-out': 'a put on; a take off; a go naked.'

The crimp who had robbed me now reappeared. He told me that Cozans and the *Rio* had sailed but if I would sign an order on the purser of the *Jefferson* for another two months' advance, which would pay the sheriff and costs of court, he would get me out. If not, I should stay and rot. And although I would now have to work out a 'dead horse' of four months, that is, go four months without pay, I gladly signed. The next day I found myself back aboard the *Jefferson*, happy to get a square meal at the mess. French Peter having charge of it that week I fared well.

Now for the first time I saw our captain – Foster, a tall, handsome man, about sixty, with iron-grey hair and moustache. I was ordered into his cabin, where he asked an account of myself. The natural austerity of his countenance gave place to the benignity of a good-hearted sailor as I related my history in a half-whimpering way. His wife, good soul, who had no children of her own, fortunately for me was in the cabin with Mrs De Costa, the first lieutenant's wife. The ladies expressed much sympathy for my hard lot, which I drew in strong colours.

And now began my life in a man-of-war. I *was* appointed coxswain of the captain's gig, taking care of the boat, and carrying messages to and from the vessel. The captain and the ladies occupied a house on Mobile Point and early every morning I was sent ashore with my boat's crew of four men. These would work about the house while I rigged a tent on the beach and took the ladies down to bathe. The trip generally resulted in my having a good breakfast with Millie, the black cook, with whom I had become a great favourite. She always saved something nice for me, while I supplied her with tobacco and snuff. She was a perfect type of the southern Dinah: clean as a new pin from the bandanna on her head to her white stockings, of which she was very proud. She did not know her age, but declared that she belonged to General Washington, and also to General Jackson, and was in New Orleans with the latter when he fought his battle. I loved to listen to her talk, while stowing away chicken gumbo, curried pig, corncakes and molasses, and such delicacies.

There were no clothes in the slop chest to fit me, so Peter rigged me out in true man-of-war style, employing some men to make my hats and canvas shoes, my pumps being brought from town. Men-of-war's men are adepts with the needle. My trousers fitted so snugly that it would have been impossible to pinch me. I was the pet of the crew, and an apt scholar.

Peter had an eye to business, and taught me smuggling. My boat's crew were in with me, and we rarely came off at night without a bladder or two of whisky under the boat, tied to a lanyard that went through the plug. As the gig was never hoisted in above the rail, we were safe from detection. Peter attended to the onboard sales, being very judicious – never allowing any man have enough to become noisy. This went on for six months in which time Peter taught me to make all splices and knots, use the compass and lead line, and to hand, reef, and steer with any man, besides all the deviltry known to the sailors of that time. A lazy life for, although we would occasionally give the ladies a sail, we generally were anchored so long in one place as to be in danger of grounding on our beef bones.

The day came Peter said we had enough money from the drink and that we should draw all we could from the purser, and desert. I had learned to love this man and would have followed him anywhere. He said that he would sham sick, to be sent to hospital in Mobile and for me to request liberty to accompany him to the city. I did so, drawing a month's pay.

Two days later we were in Mobile. Upon landing, we were met by the usual crimps, and shown to a sailor boarding house – the only home Jack knows. Well does Jack know, too, that he will be swindled before he leaves it. We were received with the usual demonstrations provoked by full pockets. We were assigned the best room and all hands were called to drink at our expense. We breakfasted sumptuously and, while we ate, saw a plan for our day's pleasure laid out. Two carriages and two large coaches were engaged; everybody was invited. By our return that evening, there had been a great deal of drinking; Peter was so helpless that he had to be put to bed. I stayed in the room with him. I had not taken any liquor, for fear of being drugged. I took off Peter's belt, which contained our money, and fastened it around my own waist. On being invited down to supper I feigned fatigue and turned in, barricading the door.

It was not long before bedlam broke loose with the usual general fight going on in the house. Pistols were used; women began screaming; and, if not for Peter, I would have jumped out of the window. The police finally cleaned out the place and all again fell quiet. I could not rouse Peter to escape and eventually, overcome by fatigue, I fell asleep. I awoke to loud rappings at the door. Frightened, I refused to answer, it was broken in, and I was blindfolded and gagged, and told that if I squealed I would have my throat cut. Taken down to a dark cellar, I cried myself asleep. When I awoke, my thirst and hunger were painful. Finally, a villainous rascal, carrying a lighted candle, said if I would ship for Havre he would give me food and drink. I asked for Peter, and was told that he would ship on the same vessel. I agreed to everything in order to see daylight again. I got something to eat, and what I thought was coffee. This I had hardly drunk when a stupor seized me, from which I only recovered under a rough shaking and a bucket of water being soused over me.

I was with Peter on board the ship *Belvedere*, Baltimore, Captain Oliver, for Liverpool via Appalachicola where we would land sixty thousand bricks and reload with cotton for the Mersey. We were told we had signed and received eighty dollars each in advance. Protest was useless; and we quickly obeyed when ordered to man the windlass, or have our heads smashed.

Upon enquiring, we found it was Wednesday. We

could give no account of ourselves since Monday. We had been robbed of money and uniforms, and were rigged in old trousers and ragged shirts. These, with the Scotch caps that we found on our heads, were all we could show for everything – money and dunnage – we had brought from the *Jefferson*. To say nothing of the eighty-dollar advance that this captain, Oliver, told us we had received from him.

To be carried or forced on board of a ship in this manner is what is termed in sailor parlance being 'shanghaied'. The word was coined in New York in the latter part of the Liverpool packet and California clipper service, when men were scarce and wages high. Many times have I seen men mustered to roll call who did not know the names they had shipped under, or where they were bound. This barter in human flesh, I am happy to say, is no longer practised.

That first morning on the *Belvedere* only six out of a crew of sixteen were able to stand up, so the captain ordered the mate to pull over to our cutter, the *Jefferson*, some distance off, for assistance to get under way.

Peter now told Oliver we belonged to her, and had been shanghaied and robbed, thinking Oliver would return us. Instead, fearful of both losing us and his hundred and sixty dollars, he somehow managed to get up our anchors and set sails without extra aid. Without passing close enough to the *Jefferson* for us to hail her, we headed for Appalachicola.

4. On the *Belvedere* men are beaten to death by officers: captain looking on. The ship declared a pest house. We help six Hoosiers desert on the understanding they will not murder the officers. In Liverpool we run out of money. About to sign in the British Navy I join the *Emily* as cook but burn the first meal. We are followed by a pirate. Peter persuades me murdering our captain and mate will save us. We make Galveston.

NOW BEGAN A three-day trip to Appalachicola on which occurred the most shocking scenes. There were but six of us who initially could do anything, the other nine sick from being drugged, or had yellow fever. I did not amount to much, as I was too light, but I could steer and I made up in activity what I was wanting in weight. Peter, though, was as good as three men, his strength and splendid seamanship standing us both in good stead. We were well treated, as all sailors are if they do their duty without growling.

We had not been out an hour when one of the crew, in a fit of delirium tremens, jumped overboard, while the mates now believed the others were shamming, and used their fists and ropes' ends accordingly.

These poor fellows were beaten dreadfully, the captain, Oliver, saying, 'By God! I'll have my eighty dollars out of them, or kill them!' Four of them did succumb, and were thrown overboard like carrion. The other five were landed, and I believe died of disease. Once the ship was known as a pest house they fumigated us, and left us offshore for ten days. Then we began discharging the bricks into barges. Of the six of us remaining, four now determined to desert. These were not sailors, but Hoosiers, cotton-balers. They had been brutally treated for their lack of seafaring skills. Peter and I decided to help them to escape. We felt we could not better our own condition by deserting at that time. It took us a week to save enough of our scanty portions of food to provide the four Hoosiers with a three days' supply of food. They intended to take the ship's starboard quarter boat and steer for Pensacola. We were to have what dunnage they could leave as our reward.

At two in the morning on the night fixed for their escape, our captain and officers were asleep under the awning aft. The men armed themselves with hatchets and cleavers from the galley, but none had firearms. They had promised not to murder the officers, although they wanted to for the treatment they had received. They got into the boat. Peter and I now edged forward to watch events. Presently one of them got out of the boat, hatchet in hand, and went to the binnacle where hung the watch to show the ship's time. This he put into his pocket. Then he approached the sleeping mate, and raised the hatchet, but after a moment turned and got into the boat again. They held a consultation, Peter feeling sure they were discussing murdering the officers and robbing the cabin. Our suspense ended when we heard them lower away. One of the falls fouled, was cut, and I heard the boat drop. All was now confusion aft. Guns and pistols were fired by the officers, but as the night was dark, and with a fresh breeze and strong current, they were soon out of sight. The excitement of this hour made a lifelong impression on me.

Our captain hailed a schooner anchored close under our stern, offering a hundred dollars if she would get under way and catch the boat. The schooner slipped her anchor, but fortunately did not find the runaways. If they had, blood would have been shed. The schooner's crew little knew the desperation of the fugitives.

When the officers came forward, they found Peter and me apparently sound asleep. We disclaimed all knowledge of what had occurred. We used the local crimps to try to make up our crew, but still sailed six men light, making the ship a floating workhouse. This we could stand, but food was short and of the worst kind. We had no vegetables on a thirty-five day passage to Liverpool. Nearly all had the scurvy. Add to this the beatings that some of the men were subjected to daily – making them on landing fit subjects for the hospitals they entered.

Peter and I worked alongside on the ship a short time in order to earn enough to pay a couple of weeks' board. Liverpool was so overcrowded with sailors at that time that crews could be obtained for American ships for the privilege of working their passage home. Philanthropists hired houses, covered the floors with straw, and dealt out coffee and rolls to the destitute sailors who had been turned out of their boarding houses. In one of these we were made welcome on paying a week in advance. With the money remaining, Peter showed me something of Liverpool. Of all the seaports I visited, I found none so filthy and degrading. Drunkenness was almost universal. The saloons were only shut at midnight and on Sundays during church hours. When God's temple on earth was closed, the devil opened his palace gates.

After ten days we were invited to give up our room. Everything except what we wore was in pawn. Then we got a chance to work our passage home on the ship *Balance*, of Bristol, PI: lying in the Waterloo Dock, loaded with salt in bulk, and leaking like a sieve. As we were hauling through the gates, the ship *Powhatan* lay at the pierhead, waiting to haul in. On her forecastle we recognised two shipmates from the *Jefferson*. They had seen out their time and signed directly on board the *Powhatan*. They had received eighty dollars each for the run and, as they avoided Mobile, had arrived with money.

Of course, they would not let us go to sea in such a leaky hulk as the *Balance* – and so we helped the *Powhatan* heave into dock and them to squander their dollars. Jack never thinks while the money is going, only moralising when hard up. He walks the streets, looks in at the shop windows, and resolves that next time he pays off he will buy this, that, and the other thing: good intentions immediately forgotten when he does land again, to be cheated and robbed as before, thus becoming a slave for life unless he can shake off the fetters which chain him to the bottle.

Dead broke again! Peter and I now had lodgings in the 'straw house', from which we sallied forth daily to look for a ship. We finally made up our minds to enter the British navy, and ship on the *Vernon*. But wandering through the Princess Dock, the *Emily* attracted our attention, battening down hatches and taking in stores for sea. There was a sign in the rigging: '*Emily*, first ship for Galveston, America'; a trim little craft of 198 tons register, Liverpool owned by Fielding Brothers, also owners of the first iron-built ship, aptly named *Ironsides*.

The captain being on the quarterdeck, Peter shouted, 'Do you want two men?'

'You don't call that boy a man, do you?' said he, meaning me.

'No, sir! But he is a good fellow, and I will make up any deficiency in weight.'

'I will take you, but don't want him. I have eight apprentices already; enough small-fry on one ship.'

However, the captain, Hamilton, had taken a fancy to Peter, whom he knew by his dialect to be a Guernsey-man, and finding further that he knew some of Peter's relations, he agreed to the two of us. I would be cook at thirty shillings a month. The apprentice who presently filled that berth would go into the forecastle.

We hauled into the Mersey at midnight and anchored. As no fires were allowed to be made on board in Liverpool, no cooking was done in the docks. I knew it would not be discovered that I was not a professional cook until too late to send me ashore. I went to the galley and met the steward – 'Bed Bill', as he came to be known. Bill, too, was a greenhorn, just out of the army. He had signed knowing nothing about stewarding or cooking, hoping to depend on the cook for his information. He wanted to get to America and believed that because he had made a good servant for an army officer he was capable of acting as a ship's steward. He paid dear enough for his assurance, of which he had plenty, being an Irishman.

Next morning was raw, foggy, and miserable. Only those who have been in Liverpool in November compre-hend why it is known as the 'suicides' month'. Breakfast was to be ready at seven for a crew of the three men and eight boys before the mast. This was to be sky-blue (boiled barley), hardtack, and tea sweetened with treacle. The cabin, however, was to have beefsteak, fried potatoes, and oatmeal (stirabout). Bed Bill was at his wits' end when I told him he must cook the cabin breakfast as I would spoil it. Six bells struck, 7am, and all hands came down for breakfast, hungry after rigging out and getting ready for sea.

My time had come. I knew that if I burned the barley I should get 'cobbed' – a punishment meted out to a cook who spoiled a meal. He was tied to the windlass and had a dozen or more blows with the flat side of the carpenter's handsaw upon his bare flesh. Few captains forbade this punishment, as they felt it stimulated the cook. Bill brought the mess-kid to the galley, and I turned the pot of barley over into it. The barley ran half-raw out of the centre, the sides burned fast to the sides of the pot. I ran my knife around the sides, and what was there dropped back into the pot looking like a man's hat that had been singed. All hands now prepared for a 'cobbing' – Bill running a line through the windlass, to be used by the crew to bouse me up. But I had some objections that none as yet dreamed of, until Bill found himself in the lee scuppers.

Peter was at my side in a moment, saying, 'Take your time, boys! One at a time; and he will accommodate you all.'

The row brought the mate, Mr Crawford, forward. Peter asked him to let us fight it out. I was at the third boy when Captain Gillette stopped the fight. As I said, I had been taught boxing by Jim Sweeney in the Mobile jail, perfecting myself under Peter on the *Jefferson*.

Now Bed Bill was ordered to take charge of the galley, while I was sent forward. Peter told the captain that I was a better sailor than cook, and that only our anxiety to get away made me ship as cook.

We had a fine run until, between the islands of Martinique and Antigua, before entering the Caribbean Sea, the weather became squally. All light sails were to be furled. Going aloft, sailor-like, I scanned the horizon for a sail. Discovering one on the starboard quarter, I reported it. But hardly I had done so, than the stranger was on us like a meteor, right astern before I'd hardly reached the deck. Peter told me to look at her carefully. She was a two-topsail schooner, the most rakish and saucy-looking craft afloat. This rig is now obsolete but if I were building a large sailing yacht, I would rig her this way. She carried a long swivel gun amidships, and a smaller one forward. She was painted black, had a flush deck, and four quarter boats. No flag was flying, there was no name on her stern, and only three men on deck. She hailed us in good English, though he who hailed looked like a Spaniard.

'What ship is that?' he asked. 'Where from? Where bound for?'

Captain Gillette replied, too much astonished at her extraordinary speed and appearance to ask any questions. He then asked the mate what he made of her. The mate replied he did not like her looks, as she appeared to be neither warship nor merchantman.

Suddenly she hove away and by ten o'clock the wind moderated enough to let us set all light sails. Then, at noon, the mysterious stranger now appeared right ahead. At 1pm a heavy squall came down and everything had to be let go by the run to save the masts. The squall was soon over, but we now had to begin to repair split sails.

About four o'clock the stranger, still right ahead, hove to till we passed, then trimmed and was alongside again like magic.

'What cargo?' he now asked.

'Coal, salt, crates, and iron.'

She starboarded her helm and hauled to southward, but before dark was ahead of us again. Supper was announced, but no one had any appetite, all sitting on the forecastle, straining our eyes to discern the schooner. At eleven the captain came forward.

'Mr Crawford,' he said to the mate, 'I don't like that craft. Trim, and haul four points to the south. We'll slip her during the night.'

Peter now said, 'If you do, they will board us. If we alter, they'll suppose we're not for Galveston, and our cargo is more valuable than we told them. Once on board we shall all walk the plank, with the *Emily* sunk in five thousand fathoms. I have sailed these waters before, Captain Gillette, and know what I am talking about.'

The captain said nothing but the course was not changed, even though the night was very dark and we might have escaped. A desperate silence now pervaded the whole crew.

Peter nudged me to follow him aft. When abreast of the gangway he whispered, 'Boy. Slip below and bring up a pannikin of rum, as you'll need courage before sunrise. For shortly after there'll be no *Emily*, or her crew, except you and me. Go! Get the rum.'

I groped my way down and brought up the drink, begging him not to take too much.

'Don't fear,' he said. 'Never too much in serious times. Here. Take a little yourself; then let us walk the deck.' As we did so, he said, 'One version of my life you have heard, but there is more. My first criminal act, a mere child led by others, landed me, and them, in the French galleys. We escaped after murdering the guards. All were re-taken and guillotined, except me – my age and my plea of 'ignorance of any evil intent' saving me, but I was sent on board a French man-of-war. I deserted for the Spanish navy, and after Trafalgar shipped in a slaver. Running from the Congo to San Domingo, with four hundred slaves, we were off Puerto Rico when a schooner just like the one ahead hailed us.

She, too, passed ahead where she stayed all night. At dawn she brought us to under her guns, and in a moment we were grappled and boarded. Part of our crew, including myself, joined the pirates to murder officers. Those of us who did this were allowed to join the pirates. We ran the slaver into Havana, where she and her cargo were sold. I stayed with the pirates three years, making my escape during a battle with two English ships-of-war which had discovered our stronghold within the great Bay of Samana, that, with its high headlands, the devil himself would select as a fit rendezvous.' After a pause, he then said 'Boy! To save ourselves we must join these pirates.' I looked at him unable to speak. 'You will take position behind the mate and as soon as they board, strike him with this knife between the shoulders.' Peter now gave me his knife, very long bladed and encased in a wooden sheath instead of the usual leather. Seeing my look of horror, he gave me more rum, and said it was justifiable self-defence. And that after we joined the pirates he would arrange our escape. He worked on me until I really felt I was doing an excusable deed.

We walked forward and I now sat on the bitts behind the mate. Peter stood near the captain. It struck half past seven. Suddenly, tears began to run down my cheeks. Mr Crawford had always been good to me; everybody had treated me well. I thought of home, and the plans and hopes I had; all to be ruined in the next half hour. I slipped off the bitts and walked aft. Peter followed me.

'Here,' he said, 'Take a little more rum. I don't think the cook will be serving coffee this morning.'

'No, Peter, no more drink. And I would rather be killed than commit murder like this in cold blood.'

But his pleadings, his love for me, and the review of our friendship, had their effect. Again I walked aft and stationed myself behind the mate.

The silence was broken by the captain saying he wished it was daylight.

'There!' I heard Peter say. 'Breaking in the east.'

The light mounted slowly, our eyes straining to catch a glimpse of the mystery craft. Again, as from nowhere, she shot out of the darkness, but now heading across our bow northward. We looked in that direction and saw a large West India merchantman about four miles on our starboard beam, Dutch from her build.

'She is doomed,' said Peter, 'and we are saved. Those poor fellows will never see the grog-pail again.'

These words were scarcely spoken when we saw the smoke from the stranger's Long Tom. This was unheeded, but the next shot brought down the West Indiaman's foremast and maintop. In less than an hour both were out of sight astern.

In Amsterdam, years after, my curiosity led me to ascertain what ships were lost the year the above incident occurred. I learned that the *Crown Prince*

William from Rotterdam, for Curaçao, was never heard from.

For ourselves, we changed our course, fearing that after she had pillaged and sunk the Indiaman, she might overtake and destroy us to avoid the incident being reported, not considering ourselves out of danger until we anchored at Galveston.

5. I join the Texas navy, desert, join a cotton gang. Shanghaied again for Liverpool – this time we turn the tables. Visit home and close old wounds. We sign in the *St Lawrence* – a haunted ship.

AT THIS TIME, Galveston, in which there were not more than twenty shanties, was the refuge for all outlaws of all nations. The British consul's wife was the only white woman I ever saw there, and the *Emily* was said to be the first square-rigged merchant ship that had ever crossed the bar. Peter and I intended to desert, but there was nothing in port except the *Houston*, a frigate of the Texas navy, and two schooners. These latter were fitting out for Africa, nominally as slavers, but perhaps for something worse. Large inducements were offered but we preferred to try the frigate.

After we had been there a week, we found a vile den whose proprietor, a Spaniard, agreed to put us on board the frigate before morning. In such a place, Peter was soon intoxicated and quarrelsome, after which came the usual general fight in which knives were rapidly produced.

I was seized by a negro woman, who hustled me outside, saying, 'I'se gwine to take you whar you isn't gwine to hab your froat cut. You were 'mong pirates, slavers dey call demselves, who is waiting to make up dair crew.'

Two negro men joined us, and the three put me into a small boat and rowed me off to the frigate, on which I was very glad to find myself. The officer of the deck asked no questions, but told me to go below, then recompensed the negroes for bringing me on board.

During the night the two schooners left the harbour but whether Peter was on board, or had been killed during the fight, I could not tell. However, by now I was glad to part with him. For although I loved him, his dangerous character always made me fear him. When in liquor he would rather fight than eat, and was always too ready with his knife.

At four in the morning all hands were piped to holystone. This done, we were mustered and presented to Captain Moore and Lieutenant Grey. Those who had not regularly enlisted did so now. Wages were ten dollars a month; time of service, two years. After this, we were stationed, then piped down to breakfast.

The captain of the maintop was in the mess to which I was assigned. He was a handsome English man-of-war's man, called Jack, with a long black beard and moustache: straight as an arrow, supple as whalebone – every inch a sailor. During breakfast he plied me with questions and it was agreed that if Peter did not turn up, he and I would chum.

At 10am the British consul came on board, politely requesting that two of His Britannic Majesty's subjects, Peter and myself, who had deserted from the British ship *Emily*, be delivered to him. Lieutenant Grey replied that the crew consisted of Texans. The consul asked that the crew be mustered.

At this, Grey said 'Do you doubt my word? The right of search will not be tolerated in the Texas service, any more than in the United States navy. If you feel aggrieved, you may report me to General Houston. Good day, sir.' After which Grey turned on his heel and stalked aft. To say that the Englishman was angry would be expressing it lightly.

At 6pm we got under way and crossed the bar, shaping for Vera Cruz. When off this harbour we hove to, in order to blockade, occasionally exchanging shots with the forts. After two weeks without taking any prizes, things became irksome so we took a stretch down towards the Caribbean. As we were passing through the Yucatan channel just before dawn, well over towards Cuba, a vessel standing the same way hailed us. It had been my watch below, so I had not seen the stranger but when I did I made her out as the two-topsail schooner that threatened the *Emily*.

'Jack,' I cried to my new chum, 'The pirate I told you about.'

Now, in answer to their hail, we ordered them to back their main yards. Both of us were on a wind heading to the east-southeast. At our order they put their helm down and tacked north. We fired our whole broadside, without doing any visible damage, then tacked after. Day was dawning proper and it became plain she had the heels of us, shots from our bow swivel falling short. She luffed into the wind as though tacking, but instead she fired her Long Tom with such effect it took away our jibboom. Then she filled, and left rapidly. Another boom was soon rigged, but by this time she was a speck on the horizon. I believe Captain Moore would have given his right hand to have captured her.

We cruised off Mexico four months, then yellow fever broke out and we soon had an epidemic. Jack had had it, but survived, and was slowly convalescing. But the disease was making such ravages we were forced back to Galveston. We anchored off the bar, not being allowed to go up to the city. A small coasting schooner had been captured a few days previous, and the third lieutenant, six men, and myself, were put on board as a prize crew to take her to New Orleans to be sold. As her crew, we were allowed to draw two months' pay from the purser. But as the treasury of the Republic of Texas was not in good credit, and as twenty-five dollars Texas paper money equalled one silver dollar, we preferred to take land warrants and peajackets instead – items we could trade. Off we went. It took three days to reach the mouth of the Mississippi and six more to reach the city, as we had no money for a tow up. So we sailed her, and tacked her with towlines when the wind failed: one of the toughest jobs I ever had.

At New Orleans, we enlisted men deserted the ship and I joined a cotton gang. The foreman was Billy Wilson, afterwards notorious as a pugilist; an alderman from the First Ward in New York; a keeper of an emigrant boarding-house; and, finally, in the early part of our civil war, as commander of a regiment to which it was popularly believed no one was eligible who had not killed his man or served a term at Sing Sing. Billy and I became firm friends.

After three months Jack was well enough to join me, and we agreed to ship on the *Sultana*, bound for New York. We were to go on board that night at eight o'clock. Wages were higher for European voyages, but I wanted to go north as I was anxious to see home once again. I had not heard, nor written, for three years. We each received a half month's advance, found a local drinking den, and that is all we knew till next morning when we were yanked out of our berths by the mates, and found ourselves on the ship *Ocmulgee* bound for Liverpool – shanghaied again: this time the crimps receiving sixty dollars each for us. Jack and I determined to make our escape, even at the risk of our lives. During the day there was no chance, as had we attempted to jump overboard we should have been shot by the mates. That afternoon, crossing the bar, we grounded and the tug left us. The mates knew they would have to keep 'watch about' during the night for fear of losing us. About 3am sleep overcame the second mate, and Jack and I slipped over the bow and swam for a large inward-bound ship also on the bar. At this ship's stern was a small pilot boat. We clambered into it, exhausted, and pulled for a Spanish fruiter waiting for a tow. Climbing on board, we begged a passage back to the city.

Next morning the *Sultana* had gone. Jack and I, together with Billy Wilson at the head of his gang, now surprised the shipping master and his crimp by appearing and demanding the sixty dollars a head he had received. It was pay or fight – and they chose to pay.

This was soon gone, and Jack and I signed for Philadelphia on the *Chester*. The voyage north was without especial incident, and I eventually arrived home. Time and hard usage had changed me from the stripling who had left, into a stout fellow looking much older than his years. My stepmother even kissed me. Her son and I shook hands, and past differences were buried in the tales of my adventures. But by the end of two weeks she was tiring of me, as I was drawing on her pin money, while my father began discussing employment ashore.

So Jack and I shipped again, and made several voyages together, or I should say half-voyages, as we deserted at every port we came to. Jack used to say to me, 'My idea is to make a sailor of you. This can only be done by sailing in many ships, and seeing how work is carried on in each; by setting and taking in sails, carrying on and reefing, handling yards and masts, setting up rigging, etc, so that when you get to be an officer the men forward will respect and follow you. I shall be a happy man when I see you tread the quarterdeck.'

To which I would reply, 'I will never go aft while you remain forward.'

'I must stay forward,' Jack would say, 'as I can neither read nor write.'

The poor fellow always felt this want. He could have been a petty officer, but preferred the independence of 'before the mast'. This was his excuse for roving from ship to ship until, in Philadelphia, we joined the *St Lawrence* – a haunted ship that had never made a successful voyage. Crews could only be found by offering extra pay, and then only the most adventurous would ship. On the previous voyage a murder had been committed and the ghost of the murdered man was said to appear during the midnight to 4am watch at quarter moons, at the starboard gangway with a sheath knife stuck in his throat.

As this seemed exactly the spice of danger we required, we signed and prepared for the voyage. I was now fifteen years old.

6. Aged fifteen – a round the world trading voyage on the ship *St Lawrence*, 1840.

THE *ST LAWRENCE* (Captain Drinker) was lying at Walnut Street, having been purchased from a Boston house by Mr Oakford, New York City, for a very low figure on account of her reputation; then chartered from him by three young Philadelphians, Messrs Welch, Lewis, and Willing for a general cargo trading voyage around the world, the love of adventure of these three inducing them to accompany us as supercargoes.

We left in the fall of 1840, and proceeded down the Delaware in tow of a tug. While towing, we had a taste of our chief officer, Mr Hennessey, noted for his brutality and foul oaths whenever the captain was out of earshot. That night, at our first supper, we spoke of Hennessey's reputation, and swore to stand by one another to the death in resisting him – to throw him overboard rather than submit to abuse, taking the oath on our sheath knives. How many captains and mates have been put down as 'lost overboard', when in reality a murder has been perpetrated, will never be known.

Afterwards, we fell into a conversation about the

murders that had occurred on the *St Lawrence* – especially the one from the previous trip, and its resultant ghost. Of course, none of us were afraid to face this ghost – only anxious to see it and prove our bravery. Suddenly, a thump overhead, caused by a dropped handspike, caused us to jump as though dynamite had been sprung under us. This jarring thump also put out the light.

Simultaneously we heard, 'All hands on deck. Brace round the yards.'

We obeyed so quickly Hennessey said, 'Boys, if you always turn out like this, I'll never need the toe of my boot.' Below again, we said we only went on deck so quickly to obey orders.

The following morning everything was set alow and aloft, and after crossing the Gulf Stream we doffed our winter clothing for summer rig. The wind hauled into the northeast, the ship spun along at ten knots, and soon we were fairly carried into the northeast trades.

The captain being a pious man, we had prayers on Sunday. But that did not stop Hennessey. We had been out sixteen days when, one evening after pumping ship, the mate, with an oath, struck one of the men with a belaying pin. The man drew his sheath knife, but before he could use it the mate struck with the pin and broke his wrist. We were about to attack the mate, when the noise aroused the captain who, with the second mate, ran forward.

Hennessey said to the man he had struck, 'Say how this was done and I will murder you.'

The captain asked Hennessey what had happened. His reply was, 'Nothing, sir. Bill here, swaying on the fore-topsail halyards, fell off the rail and broke his wrist.' We, of course, were silent.

Bill had his wrist set by the captain, and stood his watch as usual, fully determined to knock the mate on the head on some dark night and drop him overboard. This could easily be done, as he usually slept in his watch on deck on the weather rail (this ship had a very wide rail).

As there is nothing to do after dark in running down the trades except to steer, all hands slept on deck, pretty well tired out after the hard day's drilling Hennessey usually gave us. It was continually scrape, paint, tar her down, and holystone, alternating with holystone, tar her down, paint, and scrape, but we were fairly well fed.

We were now out twenty days and had more or less forgotten about the ghost. It was my trick at the wheel and I had just struck two bells (1am) in the middle (12-4am) watch. The moon was at full. I leant against the wheel building air-castles and had just made admiral when I heard a sepulchral voice intone: 'How do you head?'

To describe my terror would be impossible. Every hair seemed to stand on end, I was seized with a cold shiver, and became speechless. I tried to call the mate, asleep on the weather rail, but I could not articulate. The voice spoke again – apparently from over the stern. Letting go the wheel, I rushed forward, and pulled the mate off the rail yelling, 'A ghost! A ghost!'

The mate seemed to take my fear while the men, frightened out of their sleep, armed themselves with whatever they could seize. Suddenly a white apparition appeared to come from behind the cuddy house aft, and instantly disappeared. This was enough. All pressed as far forward as possible, some climbing out on the bowsprit.

It is necessary to digress to describe the situation of the deck houses. On deck aft, over the cabin entrance, was a house about eight by ten feet. The entrance was aft, two windows being on either side, and two on the fore end. In the forepart was the pantry, out of which, on either side, was a passage leading to the cabin stairs. Abaft this house was the skylight over the cabin. Still farther aft was the 'coach house', not seen on vessels of the present day, with two rooms on each side for the petty officers and boatswain. Behind this the paint lockers, steering gear, binnacle, etc. I am particular in describing the situation of these houses because of the tragedies that were enacted in them in the latter part of this voyage on the homeward trip.

We had not yet recovered from the fright, when suddenly the captain appeared with his passengers, all armed to the teeth, the captain now demanding of the mate the meaning of this 'mutinous conduct'.

'No mutiny, sir,' said Hennessey. 'Just the ghost seen by the man at the wheel!'

'Who was the man at the wheel?' asked the captain.

'I, sir,' I replied.

'What did you see?'

'The ghost, sir.'

'What did it say to you?'

'How do you head?'

'You were asleep! You young scoundrel!'

'No, sir; I heard it twice. Then we saw something white coming over the taffrail at the stern, from where the voice came.'

'Where were you, Mr Hennessey?'

'Walking the quarterdeck, sir.'

'Did you see the ghost?'

'Heard a voice, sir; and saw the strange apparition.'

'Right. I will now prove the ship is not haunted. You, you young reprobate,' addressing me, 'Go aft and take the wheel again. All other hands; also lay aft!'

I went and took the wheel, the crew arranging themselves around me.

Suddenly a voice was heard: 'How do you head?' The sound went through us like an electric shock. The voice continued: 'You infernal cowards! I am no ghost.' The captain appeared once more on deck.

'The ship is not haunted,' he said. 'Ghosts don't use such forcible language.'

Captain Drinker, like one of those luxurious East

India skippers, before leaving Philadelphia had had a speaking tube put in from his berth to a point directly over the head of the man at the wheel, an item never before seen, or even heard of, by any sailor on board. He had been awakened by the shaking of the sails caused by my castle-building, and used this tube. Hearing us all run forward yelling, and supposing we were mutinously attacking the mate, he rushed on deck in his light silk pyjamas, emerging from the afterpart of the house. He had gone back below – the disappearance of the 'apparition' – to awaken and arm his passengers. Even so, we were still not sure that the ship was not haunted.

We passed the Cape Verde Islands, lost the trade winds, and after much boxhauling and bracing, reached the Equator. Myself being the only one before the mast who had never crossed the Line, in order to make me a true salt Neptune would come aboard to shave me. The next morning, after breakfast, all hands turned to with the exception of myself. At six bells, 11am, Jack came down to take me on deck, saying, 'Neptune has just boarded to search for any daring to cross his dominions without being properly initiated to become a true child of the ocean, with all privileges thereto belonging.'

I was blindfolded, led on deck, and seated in a chair, to which I was firmly bound. My shirt was stripped off, and a voice through a speaking trumpet asked if I was prepared to be made a true salt. I replied I was.

The trumpet said 'Apply the brush!' This was a common paintbrush dipped into tar. The sun was very hot, so the tar, of course, was thin. I received the coat over my face, neck, and shoulders. After this the razor, a piece of iron hoop, was produced, and the shaving began. The bandage was removed from my eyes, and before me stood Neptune, dressed in long white flowing robes girdled at the waist. His grey hair and beard hung below his shoulders, and scarcely anything could be seen of his face except his eyes and nose. In his right hand was a trident, in his left a trumpet. While the shaving process was being completed, that is, while the tar was being scraped off and fat out of the slush tub applied to the parts tarred, and then wiped off with oakum, Neptune addressed me thus: 'You have now a right to become able seaman, boatswain, and ever upward to captain, if you are not killed or drowned. In the latter event you will be turned into a sea horse, and forever be my subject. You may now eat salt pork, salt horse, mush, and weevilly bread, without grumbling. I will now depart.' Through his trumpet he called his chariot to come under the bow. I was then blindfolded, and not allowed to see his departure.

Then came eight bells, midday, and we went below to dinner. It also being Saturday, we got a half-holiday for a sort of jollification and a general wash up. Mr Willing kindly furnished each watch with a bottle of gin and at four o'clock all hands were called on to 'skylark'. We climbed the leaches and luffs of sails, went up backstays hand over hand, and down the fore and aft stays. We went up the ratlines, turned under a belaying pin, walked the slack rope, and tight rope, and marked distances with the arm thrust forward under the leg. We performed the difficult feat of throwing ourselves down at full length, supported by one hand, marking with the other, and springing backward with the aid of the hand by which we were supported. We had sack races for a glass of grog, and a greased studsail yard was set upright, with a bottle of gin on top for any one who could get it. The amusements wound up at seven o'clock, when we were mustered aft, and received each a good stiff horn of grog. Such was the day in former times when a novice crossed the Equator: when sailing vessels rivalled the albatross in speed and beauty, and steam kettles, and their sailors, were unknown.

We weathered Cape St Roque, then stood for the Cape of Good Hope where we arrived the day after Christmas; which had been celebrated with a grand plum-pudding dinner. Our arrival at the Cape was a great event to the inhabitants, to whom we sold such Yankee notions as were suitable to their wants.

We then shaped for Sydney, New South Wales. At nine o'clock one morning, in longitude 73° 30', we discovered what we supposed were several small islets, but they sank upon our approach, proving to be monster squids. The only record of such squids having been seen before was made by Captain Lavender, ship *Levant*. These monsters are supposed to be food for the sperm whale, several of which were in sight.

The following day we made the island of St Paul, which was at that time uninhabited: a volcanic island, perhaps a mile in extent north and south, and about half that east and west. We hove to, to leeward of it, and took two boats to enter a basin over a ten-foot bar. This basin had evidently been a crater. Several hot springs were tested by Captain Drinker and his passengers, who used them to boil eggs, and who also hunted the penguins and gulls with which the island abounded. Outside the bar the sailors caught two boatloads of fish, as a line would scarcely be dropped before the hook was taken. In six hours we must have caught a thousand pounds of fish.

Eight years afterwards, in command of the *Manhattan*, bound to Batavia, I revisited the island, and found a Pole who called himself the king of the island, and claimed its ownership. He said he had two small schooners plying to *Mauritius* with fish, and employed twenty men. He also raised pigs, chickens, and fowls, which he sold to passing vessels.

Leaving St Paul's, we squared away, passed through the Bass Strait and arrived at Sydney. Here we disposed of three-quarters of our cargo. Sydney had been a penal settlement of Great Britain. The best society was made up of convicts, who had become ticket-of-leave men, and whose families had followed them out. We enjoyed a prolonged stay here, the ship becoming a kind of warehouse to be visited by many and various characters. Here I had contracted my first deep love for what was called a 'young cabbage-stalk' – as children of convicts were known. This young lady's father, now a wealthy merchant, had initially had a misunderstanding with the bank to which he had been connected.

Eventually we got under way for Manila. During the passage, near the Caroline group, we came across an island not laid down on the chart: a great event. We approached it, cautiously watching for sunken rocks or reefs.

Our ship had gone out armed as a defence against pirate craft that infest the China seas. This armament was four carronades and six 'Quakers' (mock cannon bolted to the bulwarks which, with painted-on gun ports, give an appearance of a sloop-of-war). We had also the usual number of pistols, boarding pikes, cutlasses, etc.

Nearing the island, it appeared to be uninhabited, and so we ran in close and lowered away the cutter with the second officer, four men, two passengers, and myself as crew. We took with us necessary instruments for ascertaining the geographical situation of the centre of the island. As we pulled in we encountered a coral reef, over which the sea was breaking. We rowed along trying to find an entrance, when we saw smoke on the island. Now we lay on our oars and waited. Three natives in nature's attire appeared on the beach, beckoning us to approach. Opinion was divided between the second mate, and the passengers, as to whether it would be safe to cross the reef. Now the three on the beach were joined by about a hundred of their fellows. The ship was now flying the recall, but we decided to stay to view these men. They were of very large stature, and a dark copper colour. Long hair stood out from their heads fully five inches, and flowed down over their backs and shoulders. How they contrived to make it stand out like bristles we never learned, but it gave them the appearance of monsters. They had high cheekbones, deep sunken eyes, and large mouths and lips, like the Patagonians

All were signalling us to approach, waving their hands towards the knee, instead of upward to the head as is customary with civilised nations.

Their numbers continued to increase to about three hundred. Finding we would not cross the reef, they, with terrific yells, took to the water and began to swim towards us regardless of sharks, of which there were many about. As the savages were unarmed, and had no canoes, we apprehended no danger, though assuming they were cannibals. Clearing the lagoon, they passed over the reef and through the breakers, and surrounded our boat, as much at home in the water as on land. So much so, that we were suddenly possessed with a desire to return to our ship. But the moment we dipped our oars, they were wrenched out of our hands. Upon this we drew our cutlasses. Seeing the second cutter coming to our assistance, they now tried to upset the boat. I was in the bow, and one of the savages putting his hand on the rail, I struck it with my cutlass. He prepared to dive under the boat to capsize her. As he did so, I stabbed him between the shoulders. But then the boat was upset, and we were all struggling in the water. The captain now despatched the third cutter, and also fired blank cartridges. These seemed to frightened the natives, who had probably never heard a gun before. The cutters' men, using their pistols with deadly effect, added their timely aid and the natives with yells and shrieks swam for shore, leaving us to be picked up by our shipmates.

Back on board the captain gave us a lecture. He said we deserved to be taken for not obeying his recall signal, and for not firing our pistols, which would have frightened the savages. The fact was, Mr Willing was so determined to land that he kept urging the second mate to ignore the recall and pull ashore. We sailors had backed Mr Willing. The second mate, fortunately, was a great coward – otherwise our fates would have been sealed.

Our captain expected to immortalise himself by

reporting the position of his discovery and, after careful observations, located this island on his charts, before we continued our course through Micronesia, stopping at some of the larger isles to trade, though never allowing more than one canoe alongside at a time. At one of these islands we were met by a hearty hail in English, calling us to heave to and give them a rope, as they were civilised. Over the side jumped a Yankee whaleman, who had deserted his ship ten years previous. He had married the chief's daughter and received in exchange a coat of the most perfect tattooing, whereby he had become duly naturalised, and invested with all the privileges of man-eating. He assured us that it was now some time since cannibalism had been practised by the tribe with which he was identified. He was, however, rather too anxious to pilot us into a lagoon, where he said we might lie and trade quietly for sandalwood and tortoiseshell. Instead, we invited them out to the ship.

A number of canoes now tied up alongside. The men wore aprons made of braided palm leaves. Shells were thrust through the lobes of their ears and around their necks hung strings of beads. The women had the most magnificent and abundant hair imaginable. It was braided across the top of the head in one flat braid, standing about four inches high, the ends falling loose over their backs, and was perfumed with coconut oil. Their bodies were smeared with the same oil, which gave them the appearance of bronze statuary, highly polished.

We amused ourselves in dressing some of these savages, Mr Willing being particularly generous in dispensing his wardrobe. To one man was given a vest: through the armholes the native thrust his legs, buttoning the garment in front. Another, receiving a pair of trousers, put his arms into the legs, and fastened the buttons behind his back. An old chief was so delighted after we had dressed him from head to foot, given his face a coat of red paint and treated him to a glass of whisky, he offered to present each of us with any of his, or his subjects', wives or daughters.

It would have required a Dickens to describe the scene, and the gravity and dignity with which the savages strutted the decks. We traded shells, yams, and breadfruit, for tin cuttings and scrap iron, of which we had on board several casks for this purpose – in those days more useful to the natives than money. For one turtle, the largest I ever saw, over five feet long, we gave three old files, a broken saw, and some pieces of old hoop iron, considered a very fair and satisfactory exchange.

And after having as much fun as we wanted, we filled away and cut the ropes by which their canoes were fastened. As this, they jumped overboard and swam for their boats, or the shore.

We shaped for Manila, arriving on a Saturday. The

ship was leaking badly, and we worked on her all day and night, and, as the following day was Sunday, expected a holiday. But at daybreak, eight launches, with double-banked oars and thirty men in each, and in charge of a pilot, were sent by the captain to tow the ship up the canal. So, after heaving up our anchor, we were ordered to breakfast, and then to trim the ship to an even keel by moving cargo. Against this we rebelled, but Mr Hennessey, with the rest of the after-guard, all armed, came forward. Fearing jail we went to work.

The rest of the cargo was now sold. Among the freight there were quantities of cider, ales, and liquors. By trimming ship we knew exactly where this liquor was situated. At noon, while the officers were at dinner, some of us went down the fore hatch and drank all we could hold. In this state we were towed into the canal and moored head to stern.

All Manila had turned out to witness so large a vessel in such narrow waters and saw us stumbling about the decks. The mate, Hennessey, now hailed the captain who was standing on the wharf with our three passengers, saying, 'The crew have broached cargo, and are drunk.'

The captain and passengers immediately came aboard, and they and the mates came forward. Being the only sailor on deck, I was seized, hustled aft, and put in irons. And old man-of-war's man, Kelso, was now put in with me, and immediately began singing the old sea refrain: 'I met Moll Roe in the morning, / And she was most happily drunk.'

I had been in this limbo but a few minutes, when the rest of the half-drunk crew came aft, led by a wild Irishman, 'Dublin Jim'. They demanded my release. The captain ordered them forward – they refused to go. Upon this the captain caught up a capstan bar and raised it aloft. It caught in the awning, and his blow was stopped. Immediately a there was a general fight. My interest was chiefly directed at Hennessey who had Dublin Jim down, beating him unmercifully with a belaying pin. I rushed forward, and with my ironed hands struck downward, laying Hennessey's face open from forehead to chin. At the same time I received a blow from a heaver, and was momentarily stunned. I recovered to see Hennessey back on his feet, face a mask of blood, calling 'Murder! Murder! A cutlass!'

Men also covered in blood were stretched senseless on the deck. Dublin Jim had the captain by the throat, head over the skylight, choking him to death. The steward came up from the cabin with a cutlass, which was seized by Hennessey. But he was too nervous, and too weakened by loss of blood, to use it effectually, and when he struck Jim across the head, he did no more than partially scalp him down to his left ear. Jim let go his hold on the captain, wrenched the cutlass from Hennessey's hand, and was about to use it with fatal effect when I interposed myself.

'Guards!' and 'Help!' had, of course, been called, and now the American consul boarded with a number of soldiers. We were all manacled up, and sent to prison.

In prison, we lived like princes on the three cents a day allowed by the ship. Our food was rice, bread, bananas, beef stew, and soup. As some men had a little money, the jailers treated us with due respect, furnishing anything from a needle to a bottle of absinthe. Naturally, we became great favourites with the head jailer who allowed us to witness garrottings, of which we saw three, and many floggings, the Chinese usually being the subjects. A Chinaman was always brought into the punishing room on a stretcher, tied face downward, to receive the number of lashes prescribed for him.

All prisoners unmanacled, except us, were employed, the Chinese bearing the worst of the drudgery. We had the best quarters in the jail and did as we pleased, usually playing cards all day. From our windows we had a fair view of the town. A bridge, with a guardhouse at either end, crossed the canal close to us. One day, as we were idly looking out, we saw a murder perpetrated. A soldier was in pursuit of a man, who was running for his life across the bridge. Seeing the guard at the other end levelling his gun, the fugitive hesitated, and was about to leap into the water, when he was overtaken and bayoneted by his pursuer. The body fell into the canal beneath. The soldier coolly wiped his bayonet, walked back, and mounted guard as though nothing had occurred.

By the end of four weeks, even this easy life had become irksome. One day Captain Drinker and Mr Willing appeared, much chagrined at seeing us idling and looking happy. We ignored their presence, anxious as we were for freedom. Drinker called me to the lobby, and asked if I was sorry for causing the mutiny, and if I would ask pardon. My reply was that he had put me in jail to please himself, and would take me out when it suited him. After further parley, eight of us were released and went back on board. I shall never forget the look I received from Hennessey. Mr Willing, however, assured me that the captain had come to a fair understanding of matters, and from now on the mate should keep his hands off me.

During our incarceration the ship had been stripped, hove down, caulked and coppered, and had begun taking in sugar, hemp, cassia, and dye woods. Now, after painting and re-rigging, we hauled into the bay to finish loading.

The Manila of forty-five years ago contained few substantial houses, these being built either of brick or stone, in the old-fashioned Spanish way. The general population was densely packed in houses perched in the air on bamboo uprights from six to eight feet above the ground, shaped like birdcages with peaked roofs covered with matting to shed the rain. Entrance was through the floor, by means of ladders. The only furniture was a mat to sleep on, and a wooden pillow covered with that same matting. What little cooking that was done occurred on the ground under the houses. Rice, bread, and bananas were the chief articles of food.

The stores were also built of bamboo. They were from eight to ten feet wide, about six in depth, and the same in height. They were opened in the morning by the letting down of a shutter, which fell outward and rested on legs, thus forming a counter on which to display the wares. The storekeepers were mostly Chinese, who made up fully one quarter of the population.

After dark few people were to be seen on the streets except soldiers on patrol, or drunken sailors on liberty. These latter often awoke the following morning in the calaboose, stripped, and in many cases badly wounded, as the natives of Manila were the most treacherous and bloodthirsty I ever saw. Nearly all were armed with a creese, a crooked, poisoned dagger, from six to twelve inches long. The life of a man in this region is of as little value as that of the fighting cock which nearly every native carried in his arms.

The Malays look very much like the Japanese we meet in our own streets. They chew betel nut and sharpen their teeth, which gives their mouths a frightful and bloody appearance. The women are passably good-looking, with beautiful black hair. Their skirt consisted chiefly of a piece of grass cloth, cotton cloth, or silk, wound around the body three or four times, and reaching nearly to the ankle, their upper wear being a loose, short smock, coming below the waist. Their feet were thrust into sandals, usually high-heeled, to keep the feet from the ground as the streets were not paved. A Chinese umbrella and fan completed their attire.

It is an old and true saying that the sailor has a sweetheart in every port, and I fell in love again at Manila. Our last day in port was a Sunday. My watch had liberty and the captain allowed us two dollars each spending money. With part of this I purchased a pound of tea and a caddy, and spent the day at cockfights, and in the evening ventured to visit my lady love. I say 'ventured', because I had a dangerous rival – a native named Lorenzo. At the entrance of the court where my girl lived was a billiard saloon. The lights of this saloon shone brilliantly across the lower end of the court, but its upper part was in utter darkness. Her house was the last of five in the row on the same side as the saloon but furthest away. It was a single room, entered through the floor by means of a ladder.

After an hour spent in smoking a cheroot with the lady's father, and in casting sheep's eyes at her, I took my departure, having been warned to look out for Lorenzo. As I regained the floor of the court I saw a figure edging along the wall, a creese flashing when the light struck it. There were also a group of five or so at the entrance of the billiard saloon. Being in darkness I had the advantage, and grasped my sheath knife, determined to strike the first blow. Lorenzo came very near me, hesitated, then, with a bound like a panther's, mounted the ladder I had just descended. I was, fortunately, dressed in dark blue dungaree trousers and jumper. Shading my face with my left hand, my right tightly gripping my knife, I advanced to within twenty feet of the men at the saloon entrance – then, having finally to emerge into the light, I dashed past them. As soon as they comprehended, they were after me.

Reaching the canal I plunged in, and they followed, doubtless thinking I would swim down to my own ship. Instead, I swam up canal to where a Dutch galliot lay, climbed her anchor chain, and was nearly brained by the lookout's handspike, being taken for a Malay robber.

I cried, 'American sailor!' and the officers and crew appeared. An armed double watch was now set as my place of refuge had undoubtedly been revealed due to the noise made by the Dutchmen.

Presently we were hailed by the port captain, a Baltimorean named Rogers. I briefly explained my troubles whereupon he kindly came off in his boat with a double guard, and rowed me to my ship. Rogers, a handsome, dashing fellow, had deserted from one of our men-of-war. A senorita, daughter of a rich nobleman, had been in the plaza listening to the music when she saw Rogers and fell in love at first sight. She became his wife. Her father was reconciled upon ascertaining through the American consul that Rogers was of a good Maryland family. Through the influence of his father-in-law, Rogers was made port captain. This post greatly increased the fortune brought by his wife, and he would gladly have left the island, but for a law prohibiting the exporting of his money, and his father-in-law forbidding the going of the wife and family. So although his heart constantly yearned for home and his parents, Rogers was doomed to exile.

What he decided to do was to put on board the *St Lawrence* his twelve-year-old son – to be sent to Baltimore to be educated while staying with his grandparents. Young Rogers was not our only new arrival. While ashore at a hotel, Mr Willing had been waited on by a Malay named Battalio, who then became his valet, and whom he now brought on board as his personal servant – plus Battalio would do some supernumerary work in the galley.

The ship was now fully loaded, and at eight in the morning on a lovely tropical day we began to prepare for sea. Captain Drinker arrived back in Captain Rogers' barge, together with our supercargoes, and several gentlemen from shore. Parting bumpers were drunk in the cabin while we, the crew, took on board our passengers – a cow, pigs, chickens, turkeys, and geese. These, though last to board, would be first to leave.

On deck to make final adieus a premonition seemed to possess Captain Rogers and his son that they would never meet again. This made their parting so touching it brought tears to the eyes of the bystanders. Then came the orders: 'Up anchor; run up the headsails; fill away; set the courses and port studding-sails alow and aloft.' We were now homeward bound. We passed the fort, from which we received a salute, while the ladies on the parapets waved their handkerchiefs. We replied with our guns and dipped our flags. By 6pm the decks were cleared and the watches set, I being ordered into the captain's watch.

The usual monotony of a long homeward voyage was broken the following Thursday at noon. The wind died, the sun became obscure, the sky darkened, the air was heavy and oppressive, and the barometer fell rapidly. Seabirds flitted around the ship in wild confusion – sure sign of a hurricane. There was no time for dinner. All hands were called to shorten sail. By 3pm the ship was snug; everything but one or two sails furled in double gaskets. By 4pm the barometer had fallen below 27° and suddenly the ship was now making two knots. At four bells, 6pm, we were sent below to supper. On this ship meals were served at eight, twelve, and six o'clock. In some ships, the mess-kid is allowed to remain in the forecastle, when Jack regales himself at midnight with a piece of pork or salt junk, and biscuits.

At 11pm, six bells, a vivid flash of lightning was

followed by a peal of thunder which shook her every rib. At the same moment the floodgates of heaven lifted, and we had to open the deck ports to let out the deluge, the scuppers and wash-ports not being large enough to free the solid sheets of rain landing on the deck. Egyptian darkness fell except for rapid lightning flashes, followed by deafening peals of thunder. Our remaining sails were blown into shreds with a noise like that of a heavy discharge of musketry. This relieved the ship somewhat, but two men on the foretop were blown overboard. The sea's spoondrift was striking like hailstones. The sea itself presenting the appearance of one great breaker, the ship was forced on her beam ends, almost motionless. The scene was one of awful grandeur not understandable except to those who have witnessed the wrath of the elements on the face of the waters.

This night's fears found some relief in the morning when the gale abated a little, yet waves like mountains still chased one another with a velocity of over sixty miles an hour. With difficulty we got her off before the wind, which by noon had sufficiently moderated to allow us to bend and set a close-reefed foresail. The ship itself looked like a wreck: bulwarks and parts of the main and monkey rails washed away, boats and water casks stove in; the galley partially destroyed, and the decks swept clear of everything except a few chickens, ducks, and pigs, which had been put into the longboat

– but most of which were drowned. The heavy strain had caused us to spring a leak and at sounding there was four feet of water in the hold. Had the gale continued we should have foundered. All hands pumped, and by 6pm we had gained a foot.

At seven bells, 7pm, it was my trick at the wheel. The crew were still at the pumps, the captain and passengers taking their supper, when the little boy, Rogers, came up the companionway to ascertain the cause of Battalio's not answering a call from the captain.

Both doors being open, I could clearly see into the pantry. The steward entered on one side, the boy on the other. In an instant, with a scream, the boy rushed out and clasped me around the body, the steward, starting towards the companionway, crying, 'Murder! Murder!'

All rushed up from the cabin. Seeing the boy still clasping me, and still screeching, the captain demanded an explanation, the steward now having fainted. Now the crew came rushing aft. All expected the ghost had finally put in an appearance. As we had started on a Friday, and this was a Friday *and* a quarter-moon, we felt that its time had arrived.

The captain and Mr Willing going into the pantry found Battalio sitting on a chair, throat cut from ear to ear. He had one gunny-bag tied around his body, and one under his feet, to prevent the blood from staining the floor. Life was not extinct, and he was carried out and laid on deck, apparently writhing in his death agonies. Having now been relieved at the wheel, I was standing at his head with a lantern. When asked why he had committed the deed, although he could not articulate, he was moving his lips and I was ordered to raise his head to bring the windpipe together so that he might perhaps be able to speak. He tried, but the blood choked him. He then motioned to Mr Willing and made signs he had left a written communication.

All this while the storm continued, with sheet lightning illuminating the ghastly scene. Now a big sea boarded, washing us into a heap. We were all more or less uninjured except my chum, Jack, who had his thigh broken. Jack was taken below and Battalio laid on the spars at the side of the longboat. No sleep for us that night; all sticking together, not one attempting to go below. Though not cowards, we felt more courageous in one another's presence, dreading we knew not what, but feeling that this known unlucky ship was still possessed of its devil.

Although pumping still continued, by 4am the gale had broken, the weather cleared, and the sun rose once more upon a fine morning. We at once set to work, the galley immediately receiving the attention of the carpenter and 'Doctor' (all sea-cooks are called 'Doctor'). There had been no cooking the previous day, but now hot coffee was served. At noon, a sight placed us on the Equator between Borneo and Sumatra. We quickly finished re-rigging sail, and received a dinner of salt beef of the mahogany sort, and yams, finished off with a rousing plum duff – with molasses as an extra treat. Duff was usually served only on Thursdays and Sundays, and plums generally allowed only on high festivals.

After eating, we turned our attention back to Battalio. His breathing had become very difficult; while the rattling noise from his throat haunts me even now. Suddenly he rose and, staggering to the rail, attempted to climb up and jump. He was prevented and now Captain Drinker and Mr Willing tried to persuade him to have his throat sewed up. At first he would not submit but being denied water he agreed, and this operation was finally performed by the captain. After the bandages had been put around his neck, he was given a drink. Although able to articulate indistinctly he would give no satisfactory answer as to why he wished to die, only showing us a document in the Malay patois that we could not read.

Being a great smoker, he now asked for his cheroot. Finishing this, he became morose and taking his head in both hands, with a sudden jerk threw it backward, and his body following – apparently trying to break his neck. This again opened the wound – a revolting sight that made us wish he had accomplished his original purpose.

The captain and Mr Willing now tried to work on his religious fears, promising that if he would defer taking his life until he were ashore, they would send his body home to be buried according to his religion. This had no effect so, it being very hot, thirst again was used to force him to have his throat re-sewn. Then, using a skullcap, the long strings of which were tied to the waistband of his trousers, we secured his head.

At eleven o'clock on the morning of the third day, he came aft and asked the captain to allow him to work. His request was mildly refused. Eight bells, midday struck, and I took the wheel. The captain and officers were below working the reckoning. The crew were at dinner; no one on deck except myself.

I saw Battalio suddenly enter the pantry and take up the knife-box; then, taking them out one by one, begin polishing them as though nothing had happened. He was not six feet from me but I dared not make an outcry, as I would be no match for him with a knife. The ship came up to the wind and shook her studding sails which brought Mr Hennessey on deck. He immediately retreated upon seeing Battalio with the knives; then reappeared with the captain, who went to Battalio and told him he could not allow him to work. To this, Battalio replied: 'I must work, or will kill myself. I cannot be idle.' From this time he attended to his regular duties, finally being allowed again into the cabin.

As for my chum – Jack, as well as the broken thigh, was injured internally, suffering intensely. The captain, with the aid of the medicine chest and medical guide, did all he could, but death was inevitable. In my watch below I waited on him, as well as in my watch on deck, the captain allowing me to go down to look after him. To me Jack showed his great and tender heart.

'Boy,' he would say, 'when I took you under my wing in the Texas frigate I felt I had something to live for. From the orphanage at Portsmouth I was put on a school-ship, then becoming a British man-of-war's man before joining the Texan service during that state's struggle for freedom. Meeting you changed me, and I hoped to live long enough to see you make captain. You were only fourteen when I taught you and now no man can match you. And though still young, next trip you will ship AB. What I have is yours. The prayers your mother taught you, never forget. Be brave, be true, and divide your last plug of tobacco with your shipmates.'

Death had no terror for him. Seeing the end drawing near, he repeated the Lord's prayer with me. In him died the truest heart I ever met. It is strange, but true, that this calamity also occurred on a Friday at 4am.

He was buried at sea, that grave that no monument can ever mark. The body was sewed up in a canvas and ballasted at the feet to ensure its descent. At noon it was placed on a plank at the lee gangway, covered by an American flag. The main yards were thrown aback to stop the ship; the bell tolling while all hands mustered around the corpse with heads bared. The captain took his place by the side of our dead shipmate, the bell ceased, and with a clear voice the captain read the impressive Episcopal service for the dead. At its conclusion, the inner end of the plank was raised, and the body slid into the ocean. A few ripples from the splash, a few bubbles from the broken water, and all was over. The order to fill away was given, and work recalled us from the sad scene. But it was a long time before I could be comforted.

We passed into the Strait of Sunda, stopping at Anjier Point, Java, where we laid in supplies of livestock, yams, bananas, coconuts, etc, plus two or three dozen monkeys and parrots, and hundreds of Java sparrows. The natives here had been spoiled by the Americans, even at this early date. They would no longer exchange commodities for tin cuttings, scrap iron, and beads. The old Spanish pillar dollar was the only thing that they would look at. For one of these we could buy from four to five monkeys, according to the size, beauty, and kind, the most costly being the 'ringtail'. Java sparrows were one cent each. Fine capons cost one dollar per dozen and chickens fifty cents a dozen. We were treated that day to a regular tripledecker chicken pot pie dinner. Then, filling our casks with fresh water, and obtaining a supply of turtles, we shaped for the Cape of Good Hope.

One of my watch, 'Portuguese Joe', had endeared himself to me by assisting in the care of Jack. As Joe had no chum – Portuguese are never favourites in a ship – my sympathies drew me towards him. During our yarns he was constantly trying to fire my ambition, saying there was no reason why I should not become chief officer of a New York packet. By applying myself to navigation, which the captain had offered to teach me, I could raise myself. And, instead of being ordered, could order others. I listened, approached the captain, and went to work with a will, occupying every spare moment with the study of Bowditch.[12]

In running down towards the Cape, Battalio became more his old self and although his throat had failed to heal properly, would talk freely on any subject except his attempted suicide. He was still obliged to wear the skullcap to press his head forward. The boy Rogers always shunned him, which was no more than natural, although Battalio seemed to have a strange interest in young Rogers. The rest of us dreaded him, and felt that Satan was saving him for some horrible deed. For though he had lost much blood, and his wound constantly suppurated, his strength appeared as great as ever. We hoped that mortification would set in with the hot weather, and end him, but it was not to be.

We rounded the Cape and shaped for St Helena, where ships of all nations stop for fresh vegetables as a curative for the scurvy. This island abounded in watercress and yams. Our stay was two hours. The United States consul came on board with letters. No one went ashore. Leaving St Helena and passing close to the westward of the Ascension Islands, we crossed the Equator and entered our home waters, the north Atlantic.

I was very fond of steering, and was considered a good helmsman. I would take anybody's trick for a chew of tobacco. This article had become scarce, as it usually does on a long voyage. I have seen a tobacco quid pass from mouth to mouth, to be finally dried and smoked in a pipe. I had several reasons for wanting to steer. First, I got clear of the dirty work, such as tarring, painting, and scraping. Then it allowed me to be left more with my own thoughts. Finally, the steward, with whom I was a favourite, would bring me various titbits from the pantry. He, too, was constantly urging me to better myself, telling me that once I became captain I could distinguish myself by my fine clothes and my watch. This good-hearted coloured man was himself very fond of dress and jewellery. He would go ashore in the very height of Philadelphia Negro style – considered the most aristocratic and fashionable of their race.

I saw him go ashore once in a long-tailed blue coat, with velvet collar and brass buttons, yellow open vest, an immense frilled shirt, lavender trousers, the very finest patent leather boots, a white hat with a green rim, a cane, an eyeglass, and a handsome red silk handkerchief trailing out of his tail-pocket. With the Sydneyites he had been exceedingly popular, and invitations from the fashionable folks were forced upon him to such an extent that, as he said, he 'had to classify them'.

Off the West Indies we fell in with a New Bedford whaler, who had just cut in and tried out three large whales. One bull yielded one hundred barrels of oil, and he got the same from a cow and a calf. If the bull is first struck, the cow never leaves, stopping by him until killed herself. The calf, of course, follows. This affection is not reciprocated by the male. If she is struck first, he immediately runs away and dives deep, not daring to come up to blow until nature compels him to.

Having arrived off Delaware, we took a pilot and proceeded as far as Bombay Hook, anchoring at 4pm. The captain and passengers went ashore to get a conveyance for Philadelphia, leaving the ship in charge of the mate. But as it would be a cold and wearisome journey, they left the Rogers boy behind.

We had just finished supper and congratulated ourselves at having arrived back safely, when someone said, 'Boys, do you know this is Friday night?' We did, of course, but did not like to be reminded of it, especially as we were feeling happy under the influence of a 'warmer' administered on the mate's orders, as even Hennessey seemed happy to be home, though still no one had ever yet seen him smile.

Packing our dunnage to be ready to go ashore the next day, we now prepared to turn in. Anchor watches had been set – two men to each – the hours between eleven and one falling to Portuguese Joe and me. When we thought it time to strike seven bells, 11.30pm, Joe went aft to look at the watch hanging in the binnacle, where a light is always kept at night. Suddenly he jumped down the forecastle, crying, 'Battalio is armed to murder the Rogers boy!'

In a moment we were on deck, and gathered round Battalio's door, directly opposite the wheel and binnacle. When Joe had gone aft to look at the time, this door was wide open, Battalio standing with crossed arms, his back against his berth. Joe had entered and Battalio had unfolded his arms, displaying a carving knife sharpened on both sides.

He had then said, 'Joe. My time is nearly up. This time I will cut both sides,' pointing to his throat, 'and then put it here,' pointing to his heart.

Joe wished to leave, but dared not turn, for fear of being stabbed.

'Joe,' Battalio now said, 'I must have my revenge. You are a Portuguese and know death awaits the scorner. I cannot kill her, so I will kill her child. His room was next to Mr Hennessey's. He is not in it but I will find him.' Joe proposed helping Battalio by finding out where the boy slept.

Battalio said, 'Go!' upon which Joe had come for us.

I slipped down into the cabin and woke Hennessey, telling him how matters were. He came on deck, cutlass in hand, and we rushed into Battalio's room. We pinioned him and took away his knife. This room had been formerly occupied by the carpenter, and everything was taken out of it but the carpenter's clothes chest. A thorough search was made for any instrument with which Battalio could do violence to himself, or others. The door was then locked and the light put out. We went below, but sleep was out of the question, as we felt something must happen before morning.

About 5am a hail came from the steamer *Ice-Breaker* – '*St Lawrence*, ahoy! Give us a line!'

We never jumped more nimbly on deck. The steamer had been sent by the captain to tow us up. I was at the wheel again, about 7am – all hands at breakfast – when I heard a noise like a scuffle, attended by a gurgling, through Battalio's door. I immediately called Mr Hennessey. He listened, heard nothing, and said Battalio was only clearing his throat. He went back to his breakfast and I was about to be relieved myself, when the steward came up with some food for Battalio. I stood with him as he unlocked the door. We found Battalio dead. He had cut his throat on both sides and had disembowelled himself. In his agony he had bitten off the forefinger of his right hand at the first joint. In the carpenter's chest he had found a pocketknife with a broken blade, just an inch and a half long. With this he ended his life.

When we arrived at the city the body was taken

ashore, and Battalio's skeleton was eventually placed in Jefferson College, where it still remains. Battalio killed himself one hundred and thirty days after his first attempt.

We had Battalio's Malay document translated and learnt his story. He had been raised by his mother who had given him a good education, intending him for the priesthood. He fell prey to worldly pleasures, and went to work as a clerk in the office of Mrs Rogers' father. Here he fell in love with her, and she seemed not averse to his advances, until Rogers appeared. Then she spurned Battalio and he was dismissed from her father's service. Then his mother died. He had waited years for an opportunity to strike. Learning young Rogers was to take passage with us, Battalio became a waiter in the hotel where Mr Willing was staying, with whom he ingratiated himself. Battalio intended avenging himself upon Mrs Rogers by poisoning her child. On that Friday night of the hurricane he was mixing his poison when a flash of lightning, followed by a terrific peal of thunder, seized him with a superstitious awe, and he fancied his hand seized by his dead mother's. At the same time his love for Mrs Rogers returned, and he resolved to put an end to his own existence rather than cause her misery.

So ended this tragic voyage. Shortly afterwards the *St Lawrence* was in New Orleans, where, through jealousy, the steward murdered his wife. In 1855 or 1856, when in command of the *Dreadnought*, I found the *St*

Lawrence in Liverpool, turned into a bark. The captain, through drink, had committed suicide. Since then I have not heard of this historically unfortunate ship. Nor did I ever learn what became of young Rogers after he was sent to Baltimore.

7. Ships I served in as officer. A good berth lost by falling in love. I find the English service does not suit me.

AFTER A MONTH'S stay in Philadelphia, Captain Drinker recommended me to Captain Fairfoul as second mate on the *Henry Pratt*, New York to Liverpool. Once there, we lay alongside the British ship, *Caledonia*, in the Princes Dock. Owned by Fieldings, she was, for those days, a very large vessel – twelve hundred tons. Her captain, Pine, had sailed in American ships, liked our discipline, and offered me the place of chief officer. My own captain said he would not stand in my way, but feared my youthful appearance and want of experience would not command the respect of the sailors. This latter doubt I told him he might dispel and, as to my experience, Captain Pine seemed quite satisfied.

We sailed for New York with eight hundred emigrants. Before we were out of the Mersey the British tars had been taught Yankee discipline, and after this all went well. The captain's wife was on board. This lady, being very proficient in mathematics, undertook to finish me in navigation.

After making New York, we proceeded to Quebec,

and took a cargo of timber for London. In passing through the Strait of Belle Isle we witnessed a most gorgeous sight: iceberg after iceberg, for a distance of over two hundred miles.

In London, Captain Pine resigned to take charge of the *William Sharpless*, an Indiaman due from Bombay. I left the *Caledonia* to go with him, but she was overdue and my money gave out. Captain Pine now recommended me to Captain Legg, *Royal Consort*, lying in the East India Docks. I joined her as chief officer for an India voyage via Australia with convicts, but did not go in her.

The captain's daughter was to make the voyage. Beautiful as a picture, she had heard Mrs Pine, who was at the same hotel, speak of me in such terms that when she visited the ship she looked at me particularly. Our eyes met, and Mrs Pine did the rest by asking me to dine at the hotel that Sunday. Her father pretended not to see all this, but on the morning of sailing day he called me into his cabin.

'Mr Samuels,' he said, 'I have the highest regard for you, and know one day you will be the top of your profession. Until then, however, much as I regret the loss of an officer like yourself, we must part company. My daughter is an only child and is all and all to me, and I cannot part with her yet. When you are a few years older, and have obtained a rank suitable to place her in, you may see me again. In the meantime, here is a document that will get you a ship at any time.'

During this interview the temperature of my blood changed from hot to cold every second. Those who have been truly smitten for the first time, and had their hopes dashed, will understand how I felt. My pleadings were useless, nor could I have an interview with her as he had arranged for her to come on board at Gravesend.

Sad and broken-hearted I left for my boarding house, and to see Mrs Pine. Only the sweet sympathetic voice of a woman can save a man under such affliction. For a few days I was entirely unfitted to do anything but mope. Then Captain Pine sent again sent for me at the Jerusalem Coffee House, a great resort for captains. He introduced me to Captain Stewart of the *Leander* loading for New Orleans, and Stewart engaged me. The *Leander* was lying in Blackwall Dock after discharging timber.

I did not like her much; she was a 'blue-nose', built as they all are in the cheapest and flimsiest manner, of unseasoned timber, iron fastened, in the expectation of being sold to the underwriters: a class of ships over which some of our western members of Congress are clamouring for us to have the privilege of flying the American flag. When we reached New Orleans I left her. The English service did not suit me, neither in pay nor discipline. In an English ship, Jack is as good as his master. This does not suit American ideas. I was in a constant turmoil with the men, they believing an Englishman's prerogative is to grumble. But we break him of the habit after his head has come in contact with a belaying pin a few times.

As chief officer I now changed ships frequently. The *Metoka* (McLarren): Liverpool and return; the *Rockall* (Evans): same port and return; the *Vicksburg*; and once more on the *Rockall*, where I met the lady who subsequently became my wife. Then New Orleans and back in the *Jessore* (Putnam); after which I married. The refining influence and Christian gentleness of my wife softened my nature. When a sailor is well-mated his wife can guide him with a silken thread, where in his single state a chain cable cannot hold him. I now made a voyage in the *Independence* (Allen): Liverpool and return; and then three voyages with Captain Edwards in the *Angelique* to Amsterdam. It will be seen that I sailed with the greatest martinets of their day, but that meant a good training among the best seamen afloat. To write sketches of the various incidents on board these, and many other ships, would fill a large volume.

8. At Amsterdam I am made captain at twenty-one. A brutal dousing and flogging. A verbal tilt with our consul at Genoa. Among the isles of Greece I race two English men-of-war. Christmas without potatoes. Offered the admiralship of the Turkish Navy. Rescue of a beautiful woman from the harem.

I LEFT NEW YORK as chief officer of the ship *Manhattan* (Carroll), bound for Amsterdam, and we arrived at Nieuwe-Diep after a twenty-three days' passage. We hauled into the North Holland canal, and were taken in tow by horses ranging in numbers from four to eighty, according to the strength of the wind for or against us. This canal was wide enough to allow the largest Dutch Indiamen of fourteen hundred tons to pass one another.

Arriving at Amsterdam itself, we entered the entrepôt dock where our crew deserted, and our captain, Carroll, resigned. Suddenly, at twenty-one years of age, married, the father of a child, I was captain of a full-rigged ship, with an entire Dutch crew, including officers, bound for

Genoa with a cargo of refined sugar. And thence for Constantinople or Odessa, as my judgment of the freight market should dictate.

But let not the young man who intends to follow the sea think that his own promotion is likely to be so speedy, for not one out of a thousand would be so fortunate, or be able to endure the rough usage I went through and lived: usages that had made me appear much older than I was. Nor do the same opportunities present themselves at this day.

The ship was now loaded. The crew were ten Dutch ABs, two ordinaries, two boys, cook, steward, and two officers. The first part of the voyage was not pleasant for the men or myself, as to drill these men to American agility produced much unpleasantness. But before the end of the voyage I had learned to speak very fair Dutch, and they to work ship in English.

Passing back down through the canal, we again found ourselves at Nieuwe-Diep, a place memorable to me because of an incident which I will now relate, that occurred when I was there as mate of the *Catharine* under Captain John 'Bully' Edwards, who would rather see a fight than eat his dinner. It was a Sunday morning. After washing down, and breakfast, all hands got shore liberty. They were not allowed any spending money for fear of drink, but Jack will always have his rum, though he sells the shirt off his back. Our crew were a pretty hard set, and proved a perfect terror to the peaceable

Dutchmen. Before long, there was general consternation in the town, and then we saw some of them being rousted back along the quay by marines from the guard ship. Our men arrived on board in a very battered condition. The commandant of the guard ship now demanded we hand over the ringleader, one Jack, an Englishman, as he had wounded one of the commandant's officers. This man, Jack, was turbulent and quarrelsome, and in liquor quite desperate, but we officers can forgive anything if a man is a good sailor – and Jack was a splendid one and one of my favourites.

After some parley with the American consul, it was decided to allow the authorities to take Jack ashore, to be returned when we were ready to sail. Twenty marines, and two officers, now came on board to arrest Jack. They had scarcely got as far as the foremast, when our whole crew rushed them with handspikes and heavers and drove them back ashore. This being witnessed from the guard ship, a reinforcement of one hundred men now boarded us, together with the burgomaster who read the 'riot act', after which, the marines divided into two squads, facing forward, and were ordered to load.

Fearing a massacre, I went forward to the forecastle to harangue the men, and Jack, on their untenable position. Jack retreated into the forecastle. The ship had a topgallant forecastle which was very dark.

The commandant, becoming impatient, ordered his

soldiers to search the forecastle with fixed bayonets. They knew Jack had a sheath knife, and did not intend to let him use it. Gradually becoming accustomed to the forecastle, they prodded berths, block lockers, and other places until Jack was discovered under the heel of the bowsprit. He was seized and eventually brought on deck covered with blood, with his shirt torn off. As he was being led aft, he freed himself, seized a heaver, and swore he would not be taken alive. He was between the water casks and the rail. I was standing on the former.

The commandant now ordered 'Present arms: take aim.' As I would not stand by and see Jack killed, I jumped down on him. They would not shoot with me on top and he was secured, taken on board the guard ship, and double-ironed.

Next morning he was court-martialled and condemned to be dipped (keelhauling being impracticable, the water being too shallow alongside), and to receive three dozen lashes. Directly sentence was pronounced, he was taken to the port gangway. A gauntline was rove through a block on the main yard, which was braced forward enough to allow the gauntline to clear the ship's side some six feet. A piece of kentledge about four hundred pounds in weight, taken out of the ship's ballast, had been brought on deck. In each end of it was a hole, through which a rope was rove and knotted underneath. The ends of the rope were brought up and fastened to the gauntline, and he was well secured between, a wooden stretcher keeping the lines taut and close to his sides. He was then placed on a grating, stripped to the waist, head and body bent down, with his thumbs fastened to the pinrail, and he thus received his first dozen lashes. The crew then ran him up to the yard, whence he was dropped overboard, striking the bottom in his descent. They then took him on board, the second dozen were given him, and he was again run up to the yard and dropped. After the third dose he was carried below in a fainting condition to be washed in pickle. His back presented a sickening sight. The blood had begun to flow at the third lash, and by the time the punishment was completed the poor fellow was nearly flayed.

Few men ever recover from the effects of a punishment like this. The victims are usually carried off by kidney disease or by consumption. The following day we were notified that if we wished we might have our man. Our captain refused to take him, but the American consul sent him to the hospital.

That such cruelty would be permitted by the staid and honest Dutchmen few would credit, yet I have seen branding and flogging in their public places for petty larceny. But I have not been in Holland since 1852, and laws and customs change in a third of a century.

Leaving Nieuwe-Diep, I felt not only the importance of my place, but also my own importance; however, I soon learned lessons about that from which I have profited ever since. With everything set that would draw, we crossed the North Sea, through the Strait of Dover, and out through the English Channel without touching a brace except to tauten it.

I established then a rule for myself never to turn in at night while at sea, except during a full calm. By daylight the shipmaster can trust his officers, but if he wishes a quick passage he must keep the deck himself at night, when it requires nerve to drive the ship to her utmost, without losing her sails or carrying away her spars. Any lubber can do the latter, but it demands knowledge and pluck to do the former.

After a rapid passage, we entered Genoa at sunrise. The scene was bewilderingly beautiful. The port is a semicircle, the Apennines forming the background of an amphitheatre; the harbour and metropolis, the stage. After shaving myself to try to raise a beard, that emblem of a lord of creation, I dressed with scrupulous neatness, hoping to impress our consul, Mr L, with the dignity of my appearance. Arriving at the consulate with the ship's papers, I was shown into his office. Before me I saw a handsome man, who eyed me at first with some curiosity, and then, it seemed, with a good deal of impertinence.

I asked, with all the assurance I could muster, 'Are you the American consul?'

Giving an Irish answer, he inquired, 'And pray, by whom have I the pleasure of being addressed?'

I answered, my blood now somewhat stirred, 'By a gentleman just arrived from Amsterdam with a cargo of sugar consigned to Messrs Giglio Brothers. And, if you are the consul, which I hope you are not, please receipt these papers and let me depart.'

This brought him to his feet, with 'What do you mean, sir? Hoping I am not the consul?'

'I mean I expected to find a gentleman, and should not like to be disappointed.'

After this, our further conversation was too forcible to be set down here. At one point he tried to intimidate me by starting to draw his sword, but little knew the history of my early training, which he soon learned.

During the afternoon, while the ship was being discharged, I enjoyed myself riding over the grounds, and visiting a grotto Byron was said to frequent, my guide, who claimed to have been the poet's valet, relating many incidents of Byron's life and habits. I also took in the grand old churches and palaces; the upper stories of the latter mostly occupied by nobles, the lower floors, in many cases, being given over to plebeians. The queerest scenes were the muleteers, managing two to four mules each, goatskins of wine slung on each side. They always claimed right of way, and took it, pedestrians turning the corner as though they had business in another street.

The ship was discharged and ballasted, and we ran out. I had a letter of credit from my owner for thirty thousand dollars to purchase a cargo of grain if I thought proper.

We passed Corsica and Elba: the former the birthplace, the latter the temporary prison of Napoleon, whose grave I had visited at St Helena. We entered the Grecian archipelago through the Cerigo channel, Greece at our left, Candia at our right. At Milo I omitted to take a Greek pilot, preferring to save the expense, and feeling quite able to navigate my own ship. We passed through the Zea Channel, entered the Doro Strait, where we encountered a 'Levanter', as the fierce storms in these regions are named. They arrive from the northeast, and last, in the winter season, about seventy-two hours. Daylight found us in the Aegean Sea under double-reefed sails, trying to work to windward. The gale increased and at noon we were under close reefs, with the current against us. Before dark we put our helm up, and ran back under Negropont Point where we hung on till daylight, hoping the gale would abate. But dawn brought no relief, the storm only increasing.

We managed, however, as the water was smooth, to keep under the Point. We could not anchor as the water was too deep, and though we were surrounded by islands, none were in sight, the horizon being narrowed to within a few ships' lengths. Night came on, and a dreadful one it was. I knew if we were blown off, we would perish. For the first time I felt that I should have taken a pilot, and that I did not know as much as I supposed I did. When day broke we were all exhausted, and I knew I must find a harbour. To the leeward lay the nearest refuge, Cape Colonna, a famous resort of Greek pirates. To reach it was fraught with danger but the attempt must be made as we could hold on no longer where we were.

Taking a good departure, we squared before the wind, steering direct for the islet of Micronisi. Negropont was now out of sight astern and we were surrounded by hissing foam, the storm being too violent to allow the sea to rise. The ship was fairly flying through the water to safety or destruction: two hours would decide our fate. A dark ridge was discovered close under our bow; its appearance that of a half-tide rock, with the water breaking over it. Starboarding our helm, we found ourselves running along the wished for islet. The mainland, though less than half a mile distant, was not discernible. Presently, the end of the islet was reached, down went our helm, the spanker at the same time being set. The force of the wind careened us over, bulwarks under. The spoondrift from the breakers of the islet blinded us so that it was impossible to see to windward. But presently the ship careened to starboard, and we found ourselves under the lee of the Cape. We had way enough to fetch into thirty fathoms, when we let go both anchors and veered out seventy fathoms of chain.

Although night had just set in, close by us, just

ahead, we could see two brigs at anchor. I could not distinguish their character, as they had nothing above the topmast. I took them for Greek feluccas. We prepared our firearms and carronades, and set the watches. I then had the whaleboat lowered, and sent the second officer to reconnoitre the strangers.

As he neared the first brig, he was met, in good English, with, 'Boat ahoy! What boat is that?' The language had never sounded so musical to me before as I felt myself among friends. They were two English men-of-war, who now advised us to give her all the chain we had. I did not wait for our boat to return, but paid out our chains to the bare end, seeing them stretch during the night like harp strings.

At nine the following morning (Sunday), though the gale had abated, I was still sleeping. I had put in thirteen hours. I was woken by the steward telling me the man-of-war boats were pulling ashore. Ordering my gig manned, I caught up with them. They were the ships' officers, as curious to know me as I them.

There is a freemasonry among sailors that meant that as soon as I jumped on the beach, we went through the rubric, 'What ship, etc?' My chief catechiser seemed to be an English gentleman and sailor, somewhat past the meridian of life, standing in advance of his group, all in full uniform.

This Englishman asked, 'Did you attempt to anchor here Friday afternoon?'

'No,' said I.

'I thought not, from the way your ship was handled, one of the prettiest pieces of seamanship I have seen. Your captain must have been in these waters before.'

I was about to reply, when one of the youngest officers asked, 'Why did you not tack ship and anchor on the bank in less water?'

This question was the sort asked by a sailor who studies by rote. A practical seaman would not have asked it. To attempt to tack or wear a ship under our canvas, and in such circumstances, was out of the question. I was about to reply to this young scion of the wardroom when my first interrogator, seeing the Yankee blood mounting to my cheek, turned the conversation by identifying himself as Sir Edmund Lyons, British Minister to Greece, residing at Athens. His brigs were stationed to rid these waters of pirates, claiming such vessels were now less numerous than when they arrived.

He then said, 'Tomorrow we leave for Smyrna, on a trial of speed between our two brigs. If your captain were ashore I would ask him to join the race, as his ship is evidently a smart one. Bear him this message, if you please. I presume you are his chief officer, though young.'

'I am the captain,' I informed him as modestly as pride, and self-conceit, would allow.

All the time we had been ascending a high mound on the top of the promontory of Cape Colon. Lyons told us that here a temple had been erected to Minerva. He was a perfect walking encyclopaedia and seemed to know the Mediterranean as well as he knew his prayers, for under Sir John Franklin he had surveyed it from Gibraltar to the Sea of Azof. His retinue were very obsequious, but that was not in my nature, certainly not at that time.

Taking off my hat, in which I had several cigars, I put them forward, saying, 'There is nothing else I can offer in return for your assistance and sailing directions.'

My youth and ingenuousness, added to my admiration, which I could not hide, seemed to warm his heart. He thanked me, seeming to know that when an American offers a cigar or a chew of tobacco, it is like the Indian's pipe of peace. I gave cigars to all present, we lighted up, and Sir Edmund went on to tell us all about Minerva and her temple. Our meeting ended with his saying they would lay off the point the next day to wait for us should we wish to try our speed against them.

The following morning, before daylight, we set all our canvas and waited for the Britishers to break ground. At 5am I heard their boatswain pipe, 'All – hands – up – anchor!' The way their chains were run in, and sails set, would have gladdened the heart of any tar. Filling away on the port tack, they crossed our bow. We, in the meantime, were heaving in.

They now waited at the rendezvous spot to leeward of the point of the island. Tripping our anchor we started after them. We luffed into the entrance of a narrow passage that had not been surveyed by Sir John Franklin. We all headed in the same direction, northward, Micronisi being between us. A fine royal breeze abeam, the sun was just rising.

With my pulse at fever heat I mounted the fore-topsail yard to con the ship through, or run her ashore. For this mad act I must be pardoned on account of my youth, and my love of displaying what I thought then as 'cleverness'. My chief officer was on the forecastle with a compass, to take the bearing of the various points I should name, with two men in the chains, heaving the lead. Presently the light blue water we were sailing through showed a much lighter patch. This evidence of shoal reminded me at once of my foolhardiness. I could almost feel the sand grinding our sides and bottom while passing through the narrow gully. Go on I must, however, as my pride would allow no other course. Now seeing darker water to windward, we luffed into that, simultaneously taking cross-bearings, which enabled us to run out into open water in the Zea Channel.

Abreast of the brigs, we put our helm up and ran under their stern, giving them the position of the shoal. Sir Edmund raised his cap, and, with their ensign run up, thanked us. The cheers that rent the air from the British tars made me feel myself a great hero. I know

now I appeared a reckless boy. At full rap we both now trimmed our canvas and headed towards Andros. We soon showed superior speed, outfooting them until the weathermost brig was on our lee quarter. Then giving our ship several good shakes up into the wind, to let them draw ahead, we kept broad off, going again under their stern within twenty feet.

Sir Edmund said, 'You have a fast ship.'

'Time is money,' I told him

'Meet me in London,' he said, before heading away to Smyrna with the usual dipping of colours, I answering with my carronade.

That night, entering the Aegean Sea, we had Lemnos on the port, and Tenedos on the starboard bow. After passing Tenedos, we closed in with the land, running along in four fathoms about seven miles from the Dardanelles, which strait I intended to enter, though the law prohibited vessels doing so after nightfall. But I thought to slip by the forts under cover of night, and was willing to take the chance.

The lead suddenly indicated ten fathoms, which proved us off the 'mouth', but I could see no entrance. As the channel formed a bend, the shore presented an unbroken line. It was two o'clock when we backed to wait for daylight. In my inexperience I had not made sufficient allowance for the current. Consequently, at daylight, I found myself in the Gulf of Zeros, about twenty miles northeast of Europa Point. After regaining my position, which took the entire day, I entered the Dardanelles, a much wiser, if not a better man, and anchored between the inner and outer castles of Asia.

The following morning, we and several others got under way, eventually anchoring off Lamsaki. The next morning was the day before Christmas, and we found ourselves among sixty vessels of all nations – Greece, Turkey, Austria, Italy, Spain, England, and Germany – all bound in for Constantinople. We were the only one flying the American flag and, with the exception of a Turkish corvette, ours was the only full-rigged ship. Our nationality and speed excited much attention, and when I landed to make some Christmas purchases, I met a hearty reception from some English-speaking captains there for the same purpose. We found nothing in this miserable mud-hole except goat's meat, which, for all the skill of my Dutch cook, proved as tough as albatross sinews. As not a potato, or any kind of vegetable could be had, we ate mashed chestnuts. These were plentiful and good, but not potatoes. Landsmen do not know what a luxury potatoes are; only sailors appreciate their true worth.

Christmas, though gloomy and miserable, was made lively by entertaining visitors from the fleet. I did nothing to diminish the reputation which Americans have acquired for hospitality, and before the day was over I was voted a 'young trump'. My vanity was further pleased when they elected me 'Admiral of the Fleet', in that I was the only captain with a chronometer on board. When I first went to sea chronometers were very rare. American ships, however, always carried chronometers, and when a foreigner saw a Yankee ship he would invariably ask for the longitude. A thorough shipmaster, of course, would spurn the idea of asking the longitude.

After twenty-seven days a slant of wind favoured us, and we led 'the fleet' into the Sea of Marmara. The only vessel that could have matched us was the corvette, which could have beaten us had she been handled by sailors. But the Turks know little of seamanship. Even less than the French, who say that those who prefer a sea life to living in Paris deserve to be drowned.

At 11pm we anchored just below Seraglio Point, leading the rest of the fleet by two hours. The following morning we started to work to windward, and when abreast of Leander's Tower, the wind hauled enough to allow us to cross the Bosporus and fetch into the harbour. But we did not come to in as seamanlike a manner as I could have wished – and if I had not brought up with both anchors I would have carried away the bridge that stretches across the Golden Horn.

On landing, I was warmly greeted by our consul. He was in company with the Pacha of the navy, who congratulated me on my skill. Our storm damage having been relayed by messenger, the Pacha now offered me the use of the dockyard, where we could heave down and have access to any materials needed. Next day we hauled through the bridge to the yard. Our men safely occupied tents on shore as there were no sailors' boarding-house masters, or crimps, to entice them to desert. We had many visitors during the repairs, which were done entirely by my crew. The Pacha visited occasionally and, when the ship was ready to go back into the stream, offered me the admiralship of the Turkish navy. I had the honour of declining, through our consul, though I called upon his highness the next day to thank him. He presented me with one of his chibouques[13], the mouthpiece of which I still have. It will always remind me that I might have become a Turk had I not been married.

Time began to hang heavy, as it does when a ship is waiting for freight or for winds to start. For, with the exception of an occasional dinner at the consulate, there was no recreation to be had. A dozen of us tried to swim the Bosporus from where Byron was said to have started but signally failed in the attempt, owing to the temperature of the water. He must have accomplished his feat in summer.

Our only resort was a hotel kept by the wife of the captain of the port. He was in exile for murder; she was a true Grecian beauty, a native of Athens, and just such a person as Byron would have immortalised in verse. Going out at night to this hotel, we always tried to walk a dozen or so strong, carrying a lantern in one hand, a pistol in the other, and wearing a cutlass. The Turkish authorities took no notice of trouble among foreigners. I once saw a Greek stab and rob an Austrian captain within twenty feet of a Turkish guard, the latter showing less interest than he would in two dogs fighting.

Between the landing stage and this hotel was a distance of about three-quarters of a mile. Most of this was a long street with gates and a guardhouse at either end. These were closed to all at night, except to sailors, who, for a few piastres, could bribe the guards to open at any time. Along this street the walls were blank, and about twenty feet high. Behind these walls were the palaces of two of the grand Pachas. Some of the windows of the upper stories overlooked the street.

One evening, walking back, one of the windows was suddenly thrown open, and there appeared the most beautiful woman I had ever seen. We were fairly electrified by her. She had defied a well-known edict in showing us her face. Instantly as she appeared, she threw something over the wall, then swiftly closed the window. It was a note. We all rushed across, but the prize was won by a Swede, Captain H, who immediately pocketed it.

At the landing stage, Captain H invited me aboard his ship. He and I were known intimates, so no one could take offence at this. Once in his cabin, having read the note, he exhibited an agitation which made him appear like a lunatic.

He handed me the note, saying: 'Captain! You are married, and we know how much you love your wife. I am unmarried, and have fallen in love with the lady we saw. Captain! Read the letter.'

The note, in a good English hand, was as follows: 'I know you are Christians, and will save me from this life of degradation. Entombed in this harem, I appeal to you to save me. God, I know, will open your hearts, and guide you tomorrow night to a silken thread thrown from this window. To this thread attach your answer.'

Captain H said, 'What shall I do? My ship is ready to sail, and as I own neither vessel nor cargo, I have no right to detain her.'

Seeing the effect she had on him and hearing him swear he would marry her if she would consent, I spent the rest of the night devising a plan of action. The first thing was to defer his ship's sailing until the dark moon five days hence. We decided he would claim to have found a leak in his ship's topside after she had loaded, which would make it necessary to careen for repairs.

Among our friends, we pretended there was no importance attached to the missive which the lady had thrown. They were anxious to know its contents but we insisted that no gentleman could divulge its contents, which justly belonged to its captor.

The next afternoon we had paced the distance from the gate to the spot we might expect to find the thread. That night, after staying ashore late, we half staggered up to the first gate, pretending drunkenness. We handed the guards a hundred piastres, and showed them our empty pockets. At this, they allowed us through, pointing to their hearts to assure us that no one should pass after us to molest us. We now paced off the same number of steps in the darkness, found the thread, and attached a note of reply. This read:

> On the fifth night counting from tonight there will be no moon and we will rescue you by rope ladder. At 1am we will attach a strong line to the end of your cord. Place the line over a hook or post, but do not make it fast. The line will be withdrawn after your descent, so none will know the manner of your escape. Before daybreak you will be on a vessel under way for England. If you devise any other means, communicate as before. We will pass nightly. May God nerve you to your task.

Now, softly pulling the thread, we felt a gentle strain in reply, and our note was pulled up. On our return to the gate it was immediately opened when we knocked, the guard recognising our voices.

The next night we received the following answer:

> I will provide the ladder. I have a trusted eunuch who will assist me, as his life belongs to me. Remember that your crime, and mine, are punishable by death. My life is nothing, but you have loved ones at home. If you change your minds, I have decided I will not

live to see another day. If you do not find the cord, I
will have been betrayed. If all is safe, the cord will be
weighted with a silken purse containing jewels to
reward you, and to assist me in my escape. If I am
discovered, be on your guard against assassination. I
shall not look for you until the hour named.

My friend, Captain H, now most desperately in love,
neither slept, ate, nor drank, nor would he give me any
rest. He was always at my heels like a shadow. As I had
thought myself the only one who could be so 'cracked',
it was reassuring to see another fellow so far gone.

The eventful night arrived. I gave a supper at the
hotel to allay any suspicion. It was served at eleven
o'clock, which meant an all-night spree. Wine flowed
freely, and had its effect on the others. At midnight, by
a preconcerted arrangement, a note was handed me by
a servant. I pretended that it had been sent by my
second officer, announcing my chief officer had killed
one of the crew. This meant immediate departure, my
friend, Captain H, insisting on going with me.

The night was dark, not a star visible. We arrived at
the gate in our usual apparently drunken condition,
spare sailor clothes wrapped round us, paid the guards
liberally, and passed through. A few minutes later we
returned and had our cigars and lanterns lighted,
pretending that the latter had been put out accidentally.
We gave them another handful of piastres, that no one
must follow us. They earnestly promised, and we

started again, our hearts pulsing. We found the cord; a purse was at the end of it, discovered by reason of its gold and silver threadwork. A stout cord was attached. We pulled gently upon the cord, and drew down a silk ladder. We put a strain upon the ladder with both our weights, to keep it from swaying, felt a heavy burden upon it, and in an instant a man in a white tunic sprang from the ladder and seized me by both arms, muttering something I could not understand. Letting go his iron grip, he took Captain H in the same manner, then sprang back up the ladder and disappeared. We were so taken by surprise we could not have defended ourselves if occasion had demanded it. Treachery or not, we did not know, but stood our posts.

Presently we felt someone else descending the ladder. This time it was the lady. She sprang lightly to the ground, and a moment later down came the man who had before descended – her eunuch. He fell on his knees, begging to be taken with us. But this was impossible. He was to be relieved by another guard at four o'clock, and his absence would signify her escape. She advised him to return, close the window, and let go the rope. She would not be missed until noon, when it would be impossible to know during whose watch she escaped. She did not speak, nor evince any terror, but trusted us entirely. We lost no time in reaching the gate leading to the dock. The guards opened it immediately. The word 'American' had a charm for them, especially as it was followed by a handful of coins. I presume they imagined we did it in our drunken fun, but it was really to draw their attention from taking too close a look at our companion, now in cap, jacket and trousers.

We made the landing place, and now pulled with muffled oars for Captain H's brig, the extreme darkness favouring our flight. My friend's vessel had two lights in the main rigging as a private signal to direct us. These were put out as soon as we reached the deck. Entering the cabin, we saw once more the face of the lady; again I say she was the most beautiful woman I have ever seen. I could not help feeling that my friend was not the handsome fellow that deserved such loveliness, yet the gods mated Venus and Vulcan. I now acted as the Swedish captain's ambassador, informing her of his desperate love, and how he was determined to save her or die in the attempt, and that I was sure that if she married him she would have a loving husband. She did not utter a word, but remained perfectly passive.

I advised him to get his ship under way at once. My boat's crew would assist him. But his vessel must be outside the harbour before daylight; and before sunrise well into the Sea of Marmara. And so we parted.

It was three o'clock before I reached my ship. Sleep was out of the question, but all young sailors live on romance and daring.

In the morning I was visited by several of the captains

who had been my guests of the night before. They had heard some sort of conflict had taken place the previous evening. They asked of the Swedish captain. I assured them that I saw him safely on board, that he was to have sailed at sunrise and, as the wind was fresh and fair, no doubt he was off. I feigned an attack of rheumatism for not going ashore that day. The following day our consul came on board, and from him I learned that one of the wives of the 'Pacha of the Army' had made her escape by the aid, it was supposed, of Greek robbers – for ransom, it was supposed. Some of these had been captured and would be executed unless they told where their captive was being held. A rigid search was made of all the Greek vessels lying in the harbour but, of course, nothing was found.

Though not pertinent to this voyage, I will here give the sequel of this adventure. Nine years later, in command of the *Dreadnought*, I was made fast at my usual berth at the foot of Rector Street, New York. Captain Hope, a Sandy Hook pilot, boarded me and told me the captain of a Swedish brig, lying at Pier 8, was anxious to meet me. Our gangplank was put ashore and a lady and gentleman came on board. I was standing on the quarterdeck with a customs officer and some passengers. The lady, whom I immediately recognised, came forward and embraced me with much warmth, and the gentleman followed suit. It was Captain H and the lady who was now his wife. After the rescue, Captain H's ship had made Falmouth, where they were married. Calling at Antwerp, some of her jewels were sold to buy the brig which he now commanded. They had sailed together around the world, but this was their first voyage to New York. Colonel Graham, now clerk of the Court of Common Pleas, who was the custom house officer in charge of my ship at that time, still lives to bear witness that he heard this remarkable tale told in my cabin by Captain H and his lady. Captain H has since sold his vessel, and become a businessman in one of our eastern towns.

9. We sail for Odessa. My ship is run down but I pay costs. Rescue of a wrecked crew.

To RESUME THE narrative of my voyage, news arrived that the ice had broken up at Odessa, and with a fair wind we started for the Euxine Sea. We would all be obliged to stop at the outer castles to send our boats on shore to have our passes signed before running out of the Bosporus, as permission must be obtained before vessels can enter or leave the Black Sea.

As the commodore of the fleet, I took the lead, and we anchored for the night at Buykotere Bay, it being too late to pass the castles before sunset. At a meeting of captains held on my ship, certain sailing directions were agreed upon for the next day. If they had been followed all would have been well, but a large Austrian ship, determined not to await her turn, came booming along at ten knots and took away our starboard cathead, foreyard, and jibboom, while our anchor dropped from the bow, and hung to twenty fathoms of chain. We were compelled to run over under the European shore, and anchor, while the rest of the vessels proceeded, but I was

still determined to be in Odessa first to take advantage
of the high freights.

The collision had occurred at 9am, but by 3am next
day I had the ship re-rigged. The crew were then sent
below for rest and refreshments, for we had had no time
for anything but the occasional glass of gin, and a
biscuit. We got under way, heading for Tendra with a
falling barometer and a storm due. During the night the
wind increased so much that we not so much carried
sail, but dragged it. Now we shaped for Odessa with the
ship running under close-reefed fore- and mizzen-
topsails, reefed foresail, double-reefed maintop sail, and
forestay sail. Under this canvas we fetched Odessa
roads, and anchored. None of the rest of the 'fleet' were
in sight. It blew too heavily to communicate with the
shore for the rest of the day and night. This was
acceptable, as we greatly needed rest. So it was 'all
hands grog and turn in.'

Next morning the wind had moderated sufficiently to
allow customs on board. Regulations were that no vessel
could enter port until she had ridden fourteen days in
the roads. This was quarantine in earnest, but the
plague was greatly dreaded. Should crucial cargo need
to be discharged, lighters were towed out and set adrift;
the ship's boats picked them up, and after they were
loaded they were once more set adrift, to be picked up
by boats from the Palatoria.

At the end of the fourteen days we entered harbour.

The Palatoria, where business was transacted, was a long, low building, divided into compartments about six feet wide and twenty deep. Three sets of upright bars separated us from anyone with whom we might communicate. Behind the first set a custom house officer was stationed, who observed all that passed between the merchants and ourselves.

To be allowed fully ashore one had to pass through the fumigating room. After fumigation, we were stripped and kneaded like dough to see if there were any boils under the skin. Our limbs then were twisted nearly out of their sockets, after which we were pronounced fit to enter the city.

One ship chandler supplied the vessels with all of their stores. For this monopoly he paid the government, annually, eighty thousand silver roubles, said to go to support the opera. This lucky individual was a New Yorker. He had not seen the American flag for many years and was as delighted as a boy when we came in; a noble fellow, generous to a fault.

As ours was still the only vessel in port, and the wind good, I held out for the highest freight ever paid. We were half loaded before what was left of the rest of the 'fleet' appeared.

Next day, a vessel was observed, with a jury foremast, steering wildly for the harbour. Near the mole she took a lurch, struck on the ripraps, and her destruction was inevitable. The spray when she struck enveloped those on shore like a rain burst near the Equator. Her crew took to her foretop. There were no lifesaving appliances and we saw the crew, one after another, lose their grip and drop into the sea. Night was coming on, and she was breaking up fast. With picked men I started out round the mole in my whaleboat to save those left. I will not dwell on our difficulties but felt fully repaid by the cheers we received when we returned. I again felt myself a great hero. Yet lifesaving crews round our coasts do this great work every gale, and think nothing of it.

The Austrian that had run into me now arrived, and her captain immediately libelled our ship. Anticipating that I would prosecute him, he thus assumed the aggrieved party, maintaining I blocked his passage. I met him by a cross-suit, and evidence was taken on both sides. His witnesses were Austrian, Italian, and Greek captains. Mine (outnumbered two to one) were English and German. The testimony was submitted, arbitration was agreed, and after a week's deliberation it was decided each ship should pay her own damage. This unrighteous judgment I was compelled to accept, as an appeal would have meant a delay of months. Each vessel also paid five hundred dollars in court costs. The lesson taught me never to sue or be sued, but to settle, right or wrong, on the best terms I could.

Now I was to sail for Flushing, Belgium, for orders. The following day I signed eight men from the brig *Jenny Jones*, wrecked ten days previous. I was glad of the acquisition, for my ship was loaded as deep as a sand barge, and we were pumping day and night. The risk a captain takes in loading too deep has cost the life of many a brave fellow. It is done to put as much money as possible into the pockets of owners, who would find fault with him unless he brought his ship home so deep a few more tons would sink her. What care they? The underwriters will pay.

I was once told by an owner, 'Captain, your ship is well insured. Take good care of her, but load her well down. Are you sure she is properly marked? The stevedore told me there was a mistake when you coppered her, and that her marks are a foot out. See, too, that your boats are all right. We do not want you to take any risk of your life, as we expect to build you a large ship in case this one is lost.' Such suggestions by owners, to certain captains, have cost underwriters millions of dollars.

As we entered the Bosporus and were approaching the Golden Horn, we were boarded by a crew member from a caique, flying an American flag. The officer had a note from our consul, saying not to anchor as he would bring out my papers.

He made his appearances in his barge, advising me to quickly take fresh provisions and square away out of Turkish waters – that my name was mixed up with the escape of Captain H's lady. In the circumstances, I deemed it advisable to lay in nothing, but immediately to show my vessel's speed. I hove off, and as soon as I was beyond observation, began to disguise the vessel. The *Manhattan*, which had white-painted ports in the morning, was black as a crow before night. All hands worked with a will, sailors being not fond of a white-sided ship which has to be scrubbed at times under very dangerous circumstances since no officer will bring his ship into port with rust disfiguring the sides.

During the night, running down the Sea of Marmara, I heard, 'Captain! Quick! A ship!'

I was on deck in an instant, but the stranger still took my toping lift over his jibboom, which pulled the bowsprit out of her. The rascal, who had had no lights, now begged me to stay, and asked my name.

I replied, 'Sound your pumps.'

On his assuring me he did not leak, I wished him good morning. I did not want another lawsuit. Having a fair wind, it was my duty to give way. And even though he had no lights, the case might go against me. Additionally, I considered my time too valuable to waste.

At daylight we entered the Dardanelles, and I ran up an English flag. I kept to the European shore, as the Turkish fort was on the Asiatic side. On nearing the fort, I took in the studding sails, as though making ready to land, and set our colours at half-mast, union down, as though in distress, yawing my ship to make it seem our steering gear was broken. In this way we passed the castles before the Turks were aware of the fact. A shot was fired but fell wide; a second fell short. We now set everything, and there was no stopping us.

In Flushing I made the best use of the time in visiting Antwerp's picture galleries, cathedral, and other noted places. These visits to foreign countries recompense a shipmaster well for all the privations, hardships, and dangers. He pities his friends on shore, whose lives are confined within a radius of twenty miles, and who are satisfied to remain at home and read, while he goes forth and sees this beautiful world.

We received orders for Rotterdam, and twenty-four hours afterwards were in that quaint old Dutch city discharging cargo. My owner complimented me upon the success of the voyage, and his appreciation was substantially expressed in the permission for me to take my family with me on my next trip.

10. Voyage to Leghorn. My wife proves the efficacy of prayer. I make relentless foes. Threatened by banditti at Pisa, we are rescued by officers from a United States naval squadron. Followed to sea we sink our enemies.

LOADED WITH A cargo of refined sugar, my wife and two children, and the pick of my old crew, we sailed for Leghorn, and thence Batavia. My owner cautioned me against extravagance, not forgetting to mention he had not insured the ship, knowing that my having my family on board would be sufficient insurance for him.

The passage was pleasant until Sardinia. Here a heavy southwester overtook us and by Corsica we were under double reefs, and had still not made land, nor could pick up soundings. The lead showed twenty-five fathoms and I judged we were five miles from Grenachi, a small island off Leghorn. A second cast showed twenty fathoms, a third fifteen, and now I wore ship. It was 10pm, pitch dark, and still the water was shoaling rapidly. We were labouring heavily, at times bow under, and destruction seemed to await. The foresail split, which eased her pitching but stopped her headway.

'Six fathoms! And a half five! And a half five !'

Any seaman who has been driven on a lee shore knows the chill that passes through the stoutest heart at such a time. Death I never feared. The true ship-master should think only of his ship. His own life should be his last thought, and if it is otherwise, he is both unfit to command, and degrades the name of sailor. But now I had my helpless little ones with me.

A sudden clap of thunder, after a blinding flash of lightning, preceded a change of wind to the northeast. At the same time a sea struck sweeping the deck, and two of our poor fellows would never more answer the muster roll.

The leadsman now cried, 'Five fathoms! Five fathoms!'

I would have let go anchors, but we should only have snapped the chains. Then the wind suddenly ceased, and the lightning showed the land to lee. The roar of the sea warned us of breakers. God alone could save us. I looked down the cabin skylight and saw my wife on her knees in prayer.

'And a half, four!'

My wife had heard me say we need not fear striking until we shoaled under five fathoms. It was now four and a half.

She came up and said, 'Fear not. God has heard my prayer. Look! A light!'

It was. Simultaneously a light wind sprang up from the shore. We set all canvas, and this steadied her, and then she began to draw ahead. Now the light, with the aid of the lead, guided us around Melora Islet into four fathoms, where we anchored at 2am.

For the first time I knelt with my wife in prayer. Until now I had let her do all the praying, thinking it unmanly.

When daylight broke, everything was changed: an exquisite Italian morning, scarce a ripple on the sea, a cloudless sky. Although close to Leghorn, an offshore breeze made it necessary to beat in. We were doing so when two feluccas came running out with signals flying. I took them for pilots. The first came alongside and asked how much I would pay to be brought alongside, adding that as a rebellion was raging, I must pay war prices. He wanted two hundred dollars. After much haggling I agreed to pay eighty dollars for both feluccas as pilots, and to take my hawser to bring us to the mole. Before I gave them my hawser, they assured me distinctly they were branch pilots.

But now, abreast of the harbour, out came an eight-oared launch, with two men and a uniformed officer, and an Italian flag flying at her stern. I was asked if I wanted a pilot. I replied that I had one.

'Those are not pilots, they are fishermen!'

The officer came on board, displayed his certificate, assumed command, and hauled us into a berth between two American vessels – the skipper of one of which, the *Lepanto*, also had his wife on board. There were several other American vessels in port, all taking in marble and rags for New York. All their captains called on me as custom, and from them I learned that a rebellion was raging at Leghorn, and that mob law prevailed. American ships and citizens had thus far not been molested, as we had a squadron of men-of-war in Italian waters, which regularly visited the port.

Now the fishermen demanded their eighty dollars. I refused, and they took me before a magistrate.

The judge, a just man, said, 'It is clear you have been imposed upon. But the city is in the hands of bandits, and I advise you to submit rather than be annoyed, perhaps assassinated.'

'No American,' I replied, 'will be forced by arbitrary power, and I look to my consul for protection.'

The consul, who was present, said, 'As the squadron is not in port, I can afford you none.'

'Then I shall protect myself,' said I.

Thanking the judge for his courteous hearing, I left. The courtroom had been crowded with Italians, all now muttering revenge. Although there were several American captains who were glad I took this stand, I was a young man, and had been too easily led to act as champion for the rights of American citizens. Had I been older and wiser I would have done as the other captains, paid up. But the spirit of our nation was in me, as it was in our forefathers, who spurned imposition and servility.

I lived on board with my family, rarely going ashore unless with other captains, and well armed. We were dogged by the fishermen and their friends, but took no notice of their threats. My ship was discharged and we were preparing to sail, when one Sunday morning the captain of the *Lepanto* came on board with his wife and suggested that we all take the early train to visit Pisa. As I never might never call here again, I consented. My wife, who always preferred church on Sunday, was opposed but was finally persuaded, wishing a sunset view of the Arno.

We arrived at Pisa at 10am, ordered luncheon for noon, then went sightseeing at the leaning tower. We returned to the hotel half-famished, entering the dining room in high spirits, congratulating ourselves upon having made the trip. Eight villainous-looking fellows entered, seating themselves at the next table, calling in loud voices for wine. It was the fishermen and their friends. To hear these bravoes clinking glasses and issuing threats made us feel some other place would suit us better. I quickly paid the bill for our uneaten meal, and we took a carriage to the baths of St Julien where we bathed in the hot sulphur springs, and now had an uninterrupted lunch. We arrived at Pisa by six o'clock, to have dinner near the rail depot.

Once more, we had just seated ourselves in this

second hotel when in walked our annoyers of the morning, calling again for wine. We again left without delay, but as the train was not due until eight, we had nearly an hour and a half to wait. Now the gang appeared on the platform – with reinforcements. Their leader we had not seen before, but a more rascally cut-throat I have never viewed. He wore a short, blue military cloak, his sword hanging a foot below it. On his head was a fur cap. He had lost one eye from a sword cut, a deep gash extending from his temple to his chin. They strutted up and down, their loud voices and half-drunken songs being very disagreeable, and we had to keep changing our position to avoid being jostled. They now numbered over twenty. Suddenly we heard the whistle of a locomotive approaching from Leghorn. As no train was due from that direction, this seemed to confuse them. They grasped their daggers, and massed themselves closely.

When the train stopped, we were astonished to see several United States naval officers, fully armed, step down onto the platform. It appeared the squadron had arrived from Civita Vecchia, heard from the consul of our court case, and that we had gone to Pisa. Knowing the state of the country, and the morals of the local *banditti*, they had at once taken a special car in search of us. We lost no time in switching to the down track, and boarded our officers' car. The cut-throats started to follow, but the revolvers looking into their faces persuaded them to remain where they were.

On the following Tuesday, the squadron sailed again. The next day I was notified by my banker that on Thursday eighty thousand dollars which I was to carry to Batavia would be ready at 11am, and that he would not be responsible after that hour. The eighty thousand was in old Spanish silver dollars. We were due to sail immediately it was on board. On the morning in question, sixty American seamen from various ships provided an escort. These, with my own crew, presented no mean force as we strode through the rabble who lined the streets watching our every move. As soon as the money was stowed, we ran up our colours, and started to haul out, and, reaching the end of the jetty, began to set sail.

I was in the cabin saying final farewells to some of the American captains, when my chief officer announced that twenty Italians had come over the side, demanding to see me. I armed myself and went on deck, followed by my friends. There, near the cabin door, stood the rascal from Pisa. I did not parley, simply pointed my pistol at his head. Even with one eye, he could see I meant to shoot him, and it was a ludicrous to see these braggarts of a few moments before, now scampering over the rail and tumbling into their boats, the boarding pikes and cutlasses of my crew, together with my pistol, proving too much.

We squared away to a four-knot breeze. About 3pm

the breeze began to freshen, and by five o'clock we were twelve miles from shore. I saw two small vessels steering directly for us, gaining rapidly. My uneasiness grew when I perceived them to be the two fishing craft that had offered to be my pilots, now crowded with men. I decided my line of action, and had two twelve-pound carronades brought aft, and loaded with grape and canister.

As the gap between us lessened, my Christian spirit forsook me, and I felt a grim satisfaction in anticipating revenge for Pisa, as I knew I could do nothing to avoid being boarded except to sink them before they came too close. I was responsible for all our lives and the treasure. I took aim at the nearest craft, now about a quarter of a mile off. Seeing my movement, the pirates dropped flat on their decks, firing as they saw me apply the red-hot salamander to our gun. The next instant louder yells rent the air as our shot took the mast out of their boat, and swept her decks. The second craft luffed to get out of our reach, but I was determined to cripple her also, to prevent her crawling up to us during the night. She was broadside to when I fired the second gun. The grape and canister did their work. Her sails were riddled and her gaff dropped. The water around was ploughed up as though by a tornado. How many were killed or hurt I never knew.

We had a fine run out of the Mediterranean and after passing Gibraltar ran close by the Madeira, Canary, and

Cape Verde Islands, passing through the doldrums with very little delay. The monotony of the voyage was broken by the occasional harpooning of a porpoise. When a fish of this kind is caught, it is a time of rejoicing, especially if fresh stock has given out. The porpoise is served at sea in a style that would put the chef of Delmonico's to the blush. Only a sea cook has the taste, or knows how to produce from this 'sea hog' the most delicious roasts, fricassees, and triple-deck pot pies. While as for the 'hash': oh ye shade of the boarding-house marm! Your house would be immortal-ised in praise, instead of execrations, if you had ever decked your tables with so dainty a dish.

Flying fish were also sometimes secured, caught in a flat net suspended under the martingale, with a light directly over it to attract them at night. But these dainty morsels are exclusively for the cabin table. The bonetta, when a school is struck, is a godsend, and clear gain to the shipowner. But Jack tires of it after a few days, and asks for his hard tack, salt beef and pork. Jack is a queer compound. Of salt beef and pork he never tires, and it is well-known that many a row has been caused on shipboard by feeding him on poultry and fresh meat. As to turtle, when I was before the mast, I saw turtles strangled to prevent the skipper from giving us their steaks, and soup, after the fourth day.

We met the southeast trades and had a rattling run to the Cape of Good Hope. Here we put in for water, as that which we had taken at Leghorn in casks purchased there was entirely unfit for use. We met the consul, a splendid fellow from Virginia, who showed us every attention. He let us see something of Hottentot life, and the ten hours passed at Cape Town were among the most enjoyable of my life. The new casks being filled, we started our run across the Indian Ocean.

On the seventy-eighth day from Leghorn we sighted Java Head. The same evening we passed through the Strait of Sunda and into the Java Sea. We shaped for Batavia and eventually anchored in its bay, amongst a sea of Chinese junks. Three of these singular-looking crafts were lying near us, riding to a hawser bent to an anchor made from the crotch of a tree: the trunk being the shank, and the limb the fluke, all heavily weighted and pointed with iron. Junk sails are of matting, and are stiffened longitudinally to the mast by bamboo, to which are laced the reefs. The rudder, a very necessary appendage, was shaped like a barn door, and had holes bored through to relieve lateral pressure in a brisk breeze, when it required the whole crew of sixteen or twenty men to steer her with a tiller reaching nearly the length of the poop. An eye is painted on each bow. As John Chinaman says, 'No habee eye, how can see?' In the after-part of their cabins, an altar is erected to the evil spirits. Upon it fruits and flowers are offered to His Satanic Majesty. They believe that God is too good to punish, and requires no offerings. At night, when the anchor watch is set, they all muster round the altar with a flat piece of bamboo, or a gong. Starting from the stern cabin, they now make a hideous racket, driving the evil spirits before them and out of the hawse pipes. They made but one voyage a year from China, being able to sail only with the favourable monsoon, and to return only with the change.

On landing I found Mr Morris, our consul, ready to meet me. Our stay at Batavia was notable for the luxurious life we led there. I felt bound to keep up a tide of American lavishness, especially being with my wife. She was the first American lady who had visited the place, and received much attention. On the recommendation of Mr Morris we were domiciled at a hotel a few miles out of Batavia. Whites did not live in the city, which was a perfect pest-hole, fatal to all but the natives, who did the counting-house work. Our hotel faced the main road, standing back about fifty feet. It was eighty feet square, one storey high, and raised six feet from the ground. It contained but four rooms, with two wide halls crossing at the centre and leading to covered verandas sixteen feet wide on all sides of the building. The east side, used as a dining saloon, faced a garden filled with the rarest tropical plants and flowers, with fountains interspersed. Here a military band played soft airs from the operas. At the back of the hotel was a stream of limpid water running over a sandy bottom, in which the luxury of a bath was complete. To each suite of rooms, two or more servants were assigned, your shadows during your stay.

Our day began at 5am when we had a cup of coffee, and mounted our horses for a ride over perfect government roads. Home again, we were rubbed down, had a bath, and another cup of coffee and rolls. Then the carriage took us to the city for business at 10am. Returning, we again bathed, took breakfast *à la fourchette*, and afterwards chatted and smoked. At 4pm a gong rang for another bath and a glass of bitters. Dinner was at six, the edibles savoury, the wines most costly. Then came either a ball, a reception, the opera, or a drive. On a drive your footman carried a large flambeau, and when many were driving the lights produced a brilliant scene. Women in this climate tend to become unwieldy and lose their beauty early in life. The men, though not drinkers, are not abstainers, but the Dutch, while too sober a people ever to be intoxicated, eat well. And this habit, in an equatorial clime, plays sad havoc with a man. The Dutchman in Batavia has been likened unto a goose in a hot oven, whose liver becomes abnormally large from overfeeding and heat. A Dutch East India merchant returning home with his riches brings also a diseased liver.

Though my orders were to await advices from Amsterdam before purchasing a cargo, I took the responsibility of availing myself of the low market and loaded with coffee, arrack, sandal- and lancewood, cochineal, some spices, and rattan. We had been just five weeks in Batavia. I did not anticipate a very quick passage home, as, on the morning prior to our departure we discovered our mizzen-masthead was badly rotted.

The night before our departure Mr Morris gave a ball of Oriental grandeur in our honour, and our start next evening was attended by a display of fireworks, and music from the fleet. At 11pm the breeze freshened, the boats of our friends cast off, and followed by cheers we ran away from Batavia. If I had remained in this place much longer, I should have had to mortgage the ship. Those five weeks cost me nearly a year's income.

We had a good run until we were within two hundred miles of the Cape of Good Hope where we caught a southwester. On the second morning of the gale I was standing between the two boats, which were turned bottom up, where I thought myself safe from the seas sweeping our decks. I had just raised my hands to my mouth to give an order when a sea struck abaft the starboard main rigging, washing the two boats and myself overboard. I managed to get into one of these boats. My southwester[14], which had been well tied under my chin, I used as a baler. I was six long hours in the water as the mate, although a good sailor, missed picking me up by wearing ship until the fourth time. Although I never feared for my life, I thought of the agonies of suspense my wife was suffering during the long hours that I was in the water.

Back on board the ship was now leaking badly at the bow ends and it took both pumps to prevent the water from gaining. With morning, the ship presented a very battered appearance. Bulwarks, stanchions, and rails were partially lost, and the cabin was nearly gutted through. But this was forgotten as the gale moderated, and we were once more happy when our clothes were dry. Sailors soon forget past dangers, and only live in the present.

We stopped the leak as much as possible, worked round the Cape, and shaped for St Helena. Here we anchored in close, letting go both anchors, and running out the chains to the bare ends to lighten our bow as much as possible, so as to get at the leak. Then we launched our spare yards as far out as we could over the stern, and filled the longboat with water. We succeeded in tipping the ship enough to repair the damage to the wood ends.

In thirty-six hours we were under way again, and in latitude 10° north we fell in with an English topsail schooner from Lisbon, loaded with wine, potatoes, cabbages, and onions. She was a perfect godsend, as we had not tasted such luxuries in six months. As the captain hove to, in order to check his longitude, he sent a boat alongside with some vegetables. In return we gave him some Dutch gin and arrack. When their boat returned, she was loaded with potatoes, Spanish onions, a keg of wine, a box of Bass's ale, and a Cheddar cheese. As I would not be outdone, I sent in return a pig, a Westphalia ham, two cheeses, and a further case of gin. Reader, if you like bread and cheese and English ale, with a mellow Spanish onion, and have been deprived of them for a long time, you can imagine our enjoyment.

The northeast trades forced us well to the westward, and we sighted the Azores. At twenty-five miles southeast of Pico, at 4am one morning, I was made the happy father of a baby girl. A shipmaster is called upon to act many parts in the drama of life: sailor, sailmaker, rigger, carpenter, painter, and, in fact, cook, doctor, lawyer, clergyman, navigator, merchant, and banker. An education that fits him for anything except Wall Street, for while no class of men understands human nature better than the sailor, none are so easily swindled.

The weather held fine, the only squall being from our 'young mermaid', while 'Jack' rejoiced when, in her honour, each watch was served out an extra allowance of grog, with a double-deck sea pie, and plum duff and wine sauce.

We made Falmouth, where we were bound for orders, and here had our bulwarks repaired. By Hamburg our ship was painted and scraped and the rigging tarred down, so that she looked as only an American Indiaman, the pride of a sailor, can look. I felt as proud of her, as I did of my wife. All sailors do, and Jack's wife feels happy in believing the ship her only rival.

It will be remembered that in 1849 cholera visited the north of Europe. In Hamburg it was raging, and in this beautiful and prosperous city Death used his merciless scythe on all. Business was nearly suspended. Among shipping, deaths averaged one hundred and sixty a day for over a week. I saw several shipmasters and officers leave on their last voyage, without time to even send a goodbye to their loved ones at home. Jack has one grim satisfaction, however: death at sea saves wear and tear on your friends. When you die slowly at home the agony and weeping is only prolonged. Besides, I would rather tussle with Neptune, and float till the trumpet calls, than lie cramped in the earth.

I paid off my crew, and sent them back to Holland. I and my family, with cook and stewardess, remained on board, using every precaution known to sanitary science. One night I believed that my turn had come as I seemed to have all the symptoms of the plague. To get a doctor was out of the question, so I plunged into a hot mustard bath, from which I emerged looking like a boiled lobster. Then I took a mixture of brandy, cayenne pepper, laudanum, and Angostura bitters, and applied a turpentine cloth over my entire abdomen. To this heroic treatment I owe my presence here!

The discharging of our cargo occupied three weeks. In the meantime I received instructions from my owner to sell the ship; minimum price, eight thousand dollars.

In fact, her stern frames were rotten between wind and water, fore and aft, but with a fresh coat of paint inside and out, and a new coat of whitewash in the lower hold, she looked the trimmest craft in the harbour. Hamburg and Bremen were the great markets for American ships at this time, as they built none themselves. Messrs Marps & Co were the largest shipowners and brokers, and Mr Marps, head of the house, responded to my advertisement and came on board to see me. I told him my price was fourteen thousand dollars, and I would guarantee her sound for that figure. He offered me twelve, which I declined. After a very careful examination, he said that he would call again. Next day, he said he was prepared to give me command if we came to terms, with the privilege of taking my family. Eventually we settled on eleven thousand dollars – take her as she lay – while selling me out of command, as he could get a captain for half my money.

The transfer was made, and I received a certified cheque. I had declined his offer of a bank draft saying I preferred cash as I was going to Holland on the mail steamer and could take it with me. After I had turned the ship over, and sent my family to a hotel, I cashed the cheque. Mr Marps now called, and invited us to dine that evening. No allusion whatever was made to the ship, just the voyage I had completed, and general shipping and freighting business.

The following morning, Mr Marps asked me to

accompany him to the ship, as he wished me to see her opened. I found a gang of men stripping some whale streaks, exposing her true condition. He complained very little, but I felt that I had got all the ship was worth, and more. I said truthfully that I did not think her so soft.

'Nor did I think myself so soft,' he said, 'as to buy her without boring.'

But he was very good-natured, and I passed the entire day with him. After a sumptuous dinner we came to business. He proposed to make me a member of his firm, saying that as the years were rapidly passing, and his worldly goods needed care, he was looking for someone to relieve him of some of his duties. He paid me the compliment of calling me 'a clever Yankee', and said that he was satisfied that I knew how to sell, as well as how to sail, a ship. I thanked him, but declined his offer. I would not abandon my profession. I wanted to see the world and become a great captain. In refusing his offer I made the first great mistake of my life.

We took passage on the steamer *Governor Van Eyke*, the first, and the only steamer owned by the Dutch at that time. Built in England, I have never been on board such a rattletrap before or since.

We passed out of the Elbe and into the North Sea just after sundown, fully expecting to be in Amsterdam the next day. But the Fates willed otherwise. The wind now began blowing fresh from northward, and the ship making such bad weather that the captain decided to lay to for the night. When day broke, the gale had increased in violence, with us crawling offshore. The islands along the coast of Holland are low and sandy, and rarely is a vessel saved when it runs aground. We struggled all day, and at night steamed at full speed to hold our own. She took sea after sea over the bow, the boats were washed away, and several of the crew badly injured. The captain was now taken sick, and went below. Matters assumed an ugly appearance, and no one knew our position as the chief officer was no navigator. A sea carried away the bridge, steering gear, binnacle, and standard compass. Now the engineer said he was in constant dread of the engine breaking down, for the ship was labouring heavily, and coal getting short.

At this, the captain asked me to assume command. I gladly did, as all I held dear were on board. I deemed it advisable to take the strain off the ship, as she was now leaking badly. So we slowed down, let go anchors, and paid out chains to the bare ends.

Steaming slowly to relieve the stress on the chains, we rode comparatively dry. At 10pm the gale broke, and by 11pm the horizon became sufficiently defined to afford me an observation. This placed us sixty miles north of Texel. At 1am we got under way, at 3am an observation placed Texel entrance south-southeast, at 5.30am we made the land, and at 7am anchored in Texel roads. We had been given up as lost.

Many boats came alongside as a steamer was still a great wonder. While we were at breakfast I heard a stampede, and found every one jumping into the boats, yelling the boiler was going to explode. Going down to the engine room, I learned that the water was low in the boilers, and the feedpipe choked with seaweed. At once I ordered the fires drawn, and opened the safety valve. Instead of doing this himself, the second engineer had been trying to feed the boiler.

When we arrived in Amsterdam all Holland was there to see us, and I was made quite a lion. The underwriters made me a handsome present and I began to feel again as if I should take my place among the great captains whose portraits decorate the walls of the art galleries. Mr Pfeifer, a stockholder in the steamboat company, was desirous for me to take a command, but I felt that the Dutch were too slow a nation for me, though during my stay of four weeks I learned to love them very much: an interesting country, which stands first for thrift, peace, cleanliness, and honesty.

11. For the first time seriously ill. I find religion. The *Dreadnought* is built for me. I reach the top of my profession: captain of a Liverpool packet! A seer in the form of an Indian princess. I battle the 'Liverpool Bloody Forties' from the Mersey to New York.

FOR THE FIRST TIME, I realised what serious illness meant. I was seized with haemorrhage of the liver, and my life hung in the balance for several days. Hitherto, out of respect to my pious wife, I had accompanied her to church, not for any spiritual benefit as I regarded a preacher as a man leading an easy life, living on the fat of the land, and only preaching destruction for those who did not support church and minister. But this flippant idea was quickly dispelled by the intercourse I had with the Rev Dr Francis Vinton from whom I learned there was something more to live for than pleasure.

Once recovered, a party of merchants subscribed to build me a ship, the construction of which I would superintend at Newbury Port. This was the *Dreadought*, and in her I reached the top of my profession – captain of a Liverpool packet! As the *Dreadnought*'s extraordinary career is sufficiently historic, I shall only dwell briefly upon some events. I had built her for hard usage, to make a reputation for herself and myself. I intended she would do her duty, or that we both should sink. I never hove her to, and for this reason the sailors called her the 'wild boat of the Atlantic'. She herself was never passed in anything over a four-knot breeze. She was what might be termed a semi-clipper, and would bear driving as long as sails and spars would stand. Twice she carried the latest news to Europe, slipping in between the steamers, and was so reliable that merchants still doing business in New York would ship goods by us which we guaranteed to deliver within a certain time, or to forfeit our freight charges – which were midway between those of the steamers and those of the sailing packets.

She became a favourite among the travelling public, cabin accommodations usually being secured a season in advance. On our first voyage outward bound, we crossed Sandy Hook with the crack packet ship *Washington*, Captain Page. We landed in Liverpool, took in a cargo and two hundred emigrants, and re-met the *Washington* off the northwest Liverpool lightship, bound in as we were running out.

The extraordinary good luck that followed us for

several years has no parallel. My success, under God's providence, I attributed to discipline, and to forcing the ship at night as well as during the day. Night is when the quickest passages are made, the best captains staying on deck, relying on nobody but themselves to carry canvas, nor did I now have to worry about my family. My children were now so numerous I thought it safer to leave my wife at home

Accepting command of the *Dreadnought*, I turned over a new leaf in the logbook of life. Swearing, which until then had appeared to me to be essential in the make-up of an officer, I now prohibited. I also insisted that the crew should be justly treated. And for the ten following years, until I left the ship, I read, or had read in the cabin, a daily service. On Sundays, these services were performed on deck with flags set, as I had begun to feel that His merciful hand was my true guide, especially after seeing his finger 'raise a dark veil' to save us from destruction off Cardigan Bay.

We had been running for Liverpool before a south-west gale, and our anxious time began when discoloured water indicated a possible sounding in the mouth of St George's Channel. At 9am we suddenly came upon a large ship under double-reefed topsails and foresails, running the same way. We sounded again, and found sixty fathoms. We used the lead frequently, and because we did this the stranger was able to keep up with us, not needing to stop to sound herself. At 1pm we sounded sixty-five fathoms, and a muddy bottom. We immediately hauled up from east to northeast, for St George's Channel and the Mersey. The last we saw of the stranger she was still holding her course. At 3pm the weather cleared for a moment, when St David's Head (Wales) loomed close on our starboard bow. I remarked to the mate that if the stranger held his course, he would run ashore back of the Bishop's Rocks. After passing St David's Head, we shaped to pass three miles off Holyhead, whose light I expected to see by 7pm. That evening we had our service at six o'clock instead of eight, so that I could be back on deck.

I had scarcely closed the prayer book when the dense fog miraculously lifted for a moment and I heard 'Light on the port bow!'

There was not a moment to be lost hauling up to clear the land. Here God's mercy was clearly shown, for had not the thick veil lifted to let me catch a glimpse of the light, the *Dreadnought* would have been wrecked in less than five minutes.

As for the stranger, the day after arriving in Liverpool, and tying up as usual in the Waterloo Dock, we learned that on the night in question the ship *Grand Duce* (Sampson) from New Orleans, bound to Liverpool with cotton, was lost with all hands, except for two men saved on a bale. The foregoing is a warning that the use of the 'blue pigeon', the deep-sea lead, should never be neglected, however sure we may be of our position.

At the time of which I write, the American flag predominated in the docks of Liverpool. American shipping furnished the city with food supplies, and with cotton for her factories. The impetus given to Liverpool by American industry made her the second, if not the first and greatest, seaport in the world.

A few trips later we left Sandy Hook in the middle of February, so cold that eight of our men were frostbitten the first night out. We were driving hard, the decks and rigging a mass of ice. We were making the northern passage, to be sure of having wind enough. In seventy-two hours from Sandy Hook we sailed 1080 miles. Had the wind continued we would have made Liverpool in under nine days. At the tea table I was congratulated by the passengers, among whom was an Indian princess, a daughter of Osceola[15], so she said, going to visit the Queen of England, whom she claimed as her cousin.

I had my doubts of her pure Indian lineage from the size of her lips and kinky hair, but upon the whole she was not bad-looking, with her coffee-coloured skin, and lips and cheeks tinged with carmine. She wore a fantastic dress, and was extremely dignified in her carriage. She was not troubled with seasickness, and was therefore able to devote much of her time to me, when I heard of her wonderful power as a medicine woman and a seer. She would sometimes close her eyes and predict our landing in England, and her reception at

Buckingham Palace, after we had made a record-breaking run of eight days. She declared that she bore a charmed life, and that, wherever she might be, from that place dangers were warded off.

One day in the cabin, listening to one of her fancies, I heard the cry, 'Breakers ahead!' It had just struck eight bells, we were logging fourteen and a half knots, the air temperature was 30°F, the sea, 34°F. These reported breakers I knew to be field ice. The helm was put hard a-port to get our head to the southward, to meet any ice 'beam on', to avoid the shock of running our prow into it. Soon we were well into the field, the scene being grand, but fearful. As far as the eye could reach there seemed one vast sea of ice, the light from which made the sky seem inky black. I deemed it advisable to work the ship out, as the weight of the ice kept the sea down, except for a slight undulating motion, though forcing her through made her tremble in all her timbers.

The princess, most frightened of all the passengers, clambered into one of the quarter-boats, where she remained until we left the pack about 3am. I then assisted her into the cabin, where a good stiff horn of 'firewater' was administered to her. She was very grateful, and believed a second dose would quite restore her, which it did.

Next morning, at the breakfast table, I asked, 'Why did you not let me know you had foreseen this event? I could have taken a more southerly course.'

'Small matters I do not notice,' she said.

'May we expect any further unpleasantness?'

'None,' she replied.

During the day the wind hauled to eastward, and by 10pm we were standing on a starboard tack heading northeast. I went below at midnight, leaving my chief officer, a first-class man, on the deck. I heard him order the helm hard up, and at the same time felt the ship careen to windward. I jumped on deck and found a large ship, with no lights, running down on us. A collision was inevitable. Her lookout must have been asleep, as our lights were burning brightly. We would have crossed her bow had she kept her course, but when they finally saw us coming they became confused, and instead of starboarding, ported her helm. Our starboard bow took her port bow, giving her a glancing blow.

By this time her sails were aback, and our head had paid off enough for us to receive a second blow from her. Their crew now tried to jump on board of us, saying they were sinking. Another blow took us aft of the mizzen rigging, as we both came down into the hollow of the sea. We knocked a hole in his port counter large enough to drive a wagon through. We parted again on the rise of the sea, he now sweeping away our starboard rail, stanchions, mizzen-topgallant mast and everything attached to it. In answer to his cries to lay by him, as he was sinking, we shortened canvas and hove to, to pick up his crew, keeping torches burning to show our position. We lost sight of him at three o'clock, and I supposed he had sunk, and his boats would board us. We lay to till daylight, but saw no more of him. We had no time to ask the name of his ship, nor he ours.

At the time of the collision the princess appeared upon the scene. I was too busy with my crew, who were rather demoralised, to be very courteous to her. At the second collision she prepared to leave the ship. She climbed into the boat wearing only her nightgown. She had a pillow under each arm. (Afterwards she told me that she considered feathers as good for life-preservers as cork, and much lighter.) Nothing could induce her to get out of the boat before daylight so I had some blankets thrown over her to keep her from freezing. She attributed her loss of prophesying powers to being on the ocean, where 'the red man never treads'. She also told me she would never cross the sea again. At this, I informed her that she would have to find her way back via the North Pole. And although it would be a cool trip, the chances of solid footing were much better there than along the usual route.

Two or three voyages after this, I picked up an old Liverpool paper and read that the ship *Eugenie* (London for Quebec) had been run into by a large Yankee packet, which did not stop but left the *Eugenie*, and all its hands, to sink from a hole in her stern. I was so indignant that I was going to sue for damages to expose *his* cowardice, but recalled the vow I made after the incident in Odessa.

During the above action, I mentioned demoralisation among the crew. The Liverpool packet sailor was not easily demoralised, being the toughest class of men in all respects. They could stand the worst weather, food, and usage, and put up with less sleep, more rum, and harder knocks than any other sailors on earth. They would not sail in any other trade. They had not the slightest idea of morality or honesty, and gratitude was not in them. Only the belaying pin or heaver could keep them in subjection. At times, I tried to humanise their brutal natures, but the better they were treated the more trouble they gave. They came on board, winter and summer, with what covered them, though always with an empty bag.

At the end of the run, these bags would be full of what they had stolen from unfortunate shipmates who were on a packet for the first time, unfortunates who were always frightened to say who had stolen their clothes – even if they knew. Sometimes I would notice these hard cases getting stouter and stouter until there was not an article of clothing left in the forecastle. Then I would call all hands aft and make them strip to their underclothing, and mix the clothes in a heap. Then, one by one, those who had been robbed were allowed to select what they had lost. The 'packetarians' were always invited last, and they invariably found themselves reduced to the same toggery in which they boarded. Having said this, they were undoubtedly the toughest and best sailors.

Once, however, I could not find where they hid their plunder, until as we were docking I missed two of them from the capstan. It was not quite light, and I slipped from the cabin through the steerage, and up the fore hatch on the port side. I found two of them straddling a water cask, fishing plunder out of it. It was a queer place to hide clothes, in the water we drank. I had had a large square hole cut in our water cask instead of a bunghole, in order to break the ice as it formed in the casks in severe weather, for the expansion would have otherwise destroyed them.

There was one particular group, the 'Liverpool Bloody Forties', consummate rascals who were dead to any moral suasion, as the following account attests. It fell to my lot to ship thirty of these at the same time, their number presently in Liverpool. Justice Mansfield, who used to send me boys in whom he thought there were some good traits (instead of sending them to jail), and some of whom grew into excellent officers, manifested much interest when he heard that thirty of the 'Bloodies' were going with me. He told me that his detectives had unearthed a plot hatched in Ma Riley's den, and that their leaders, Finnigan, Casey and Sweeney, intended to have me 'holystoning in hell' before we reached New York. The previous winter, these three had been part of the crew on the *Columbia* when poor Captain Bryer had been murdered.

Sailing day arrived, 11 July 1859. We were anchored in the Mersey, ready for sea, emigrants and passengers safely stowed. Captain Shomburg, the emigrant agent, came on board to give me my final clearances. Taking one look at the crew, he said, 'I've never seen such a set in my life, and advise you not to take them.'

'I will draw their teeth,' said I, patting the head of Wallace, my Newfoundland dog, who stood beside me. I called the crew aft.

'Men,' I said. 'You know the rules. Pass by the carpenter shop and have the ends of your knives broken.'

'What for?' asked Sweeney.

'Another word,' I told him, 'And I'll have you against the shrouds!' This was greeted by hisses. But on me repeating 'You heard the order!' it was done, but with so many grumblings, that I again ordered, 'Lay aft all hands!'

They came in a sort of dogged, insolent manner.

'Men,' I now said, 'The manner you assumed just now is insulting. And you know it! Finnigan! Casey! Sweeney! I know you took an oath in Mrs Riley's to clip the wings of the *Dreadnought*, and give her skipper a swim – as you think the lid of Davy Jones's locker has been open for me long enough! Well! I am glad to have you with me as I think I can teach you a lesson that will last you through life. Sweeney, you and I were together in Mobile jail. What was in me there as a boy is now fully developed in me as a man, but thankfully divested of the villainous associations. Now! Stand where you are while the officers search you for hidden weapons.'

After this had been done, and the forecastle searched, I told them, 'According to your behaviour you shall have watch and watch, and an occasional glass of grog.' Then I relented. 'And as I see some of you shivering for want of it, you shall have one now.'

After this, they manned the windlass, the anchor was hove, and the tug took us as far as Point Lynas. With a moderate breeze we stood across the Channel to the Irish shore, then tacked again, and worked down with a steady breeze from westward. The next morning, 12 July 1859, at 4am, we tacked close to St David's Head, and I gave the order to put the helm down. This the man at the wheel did – but without repeating the order.

My next order was 'Hard a-lee!' At this time the head sheets should be let go. This was not done, nearly causing the ship to mis-stay. The next order was, 'Raise tacks and sheets', then 'Haul taut the weather mainbrace.'

This was done – but slowly. I called all hands aft, and gave those responsible a sharp reprimand, while the man at the wheel was told to repeat all orders. At noon, off Queenstown, while the crew were at dinner, I was walking the quarterdeck with Wallace when I noticed the man at the wheel steering unsteadily.

I said, 'Steer steady!' He made no reply. 'Did you hear me speak to you, sir?'

'I am steering steady,' he answered in a sullen manner.

His impertinent tone caused me to jump towards him. He attempted to draw his knife, but I struck him senseless. Wallace now took charge, keeping his forepaws on the man's chest, while I handcuffed him. I took up his knife. It had been repointed, which led me to believe that so would all the others be. The man was locked in the afterhouse. This scene was enacted so quickly that the crew knew nothing of it, except what they heard from some passengers immediately after.

The second mate took the wheel until two bells, one o'clock, at which time, the crew being back from dinner, the order was given, 'Turn to and haul taut the weather mainbrace.' Instead, they came aft to the quarterdeck. 'Why don't you obey the order?' I asked.

'Let Mike out of irons,' was the reply.

'Men!' I said, 'It is time you learned who is master. For I see kind treatment will not prevail. For the remainder of the voyage I shall stop your watch and watch, and treat you as you deserve. Again I repeat, haul taut the weather mainbrace! Understand a refusal to obey puts you in mutiny!'

Not a man moved. The emigrants, who were not allowed on the quarterdeck, were all huddling near the mainmast, wondering what would happen.

Now, as the mutineers ran forward to the forecastle, I turned into the cabin to arm myself. When I came out I had on a raglan to conceal my weapons. I ordered the emigrants to go below, and called my officers, and the carpenter and cook, into the cabin. I told them we were six against thirty – and asked how they stood. The mate, Parker, told me he would do no fighting.

'Then, you cur, you're no officer of mine!'

The second, Mr Whitehorn, saluted, and said, 'You know me, Captain.'

The third mate, Hooker, said 'I'm afraid I'm a little old ...' I told him and Parker to report to the galley. This left the carpenter and cook.

'Well,' I said. 'What can I expect?'

The cook, big and fat, slapped his hand on his stomach as if say, 'this would get in the way.' The carpenter said he did not sign on to fight, and fight he would not.

This left myself, and Mr Whitehorn, and the boys. Mr Whitehorn had been with me for many years, and, though small in stature, was as brave as a lion. I asked him to take the wheel while I went forward with Wallace. I reached the galley door, about six feet from the forward end of the house. The passage which I had traversed between the water cask and the rail was less than five feet wide. I was still advancing when, with yells like demons let loose, the crew came round the back of the house and rushed at me with their knives.

With a pistol in each hand, and a cutlass at my side, I stood immovable. Wallace barking furiously. All stopped dead.

Into the silence, I said, 'Men, you have found your master.' Still finding they would not listen, I half turned to retreat, when, with more fierce yells, they attempted to rush me. Wheeling once more, I cried, 'The first to take another step dies!' Then, backing through the passage-way as far as the main hatch, I turned and walked aft.

During all this, the screaming of the emigrant women and children below, blended with the noise on deck, and Wallace's continuous barking, beggars all description. The Norwegians were praying one kind of prayer, the Germans another, the Hungarians singing theirs. In the cabin, the steward told me later, our only female passenger, the wife of a prominent New York attorney, went missing – discovered two hours later hiding under a couch. During the afternoon, other passengers now came to request me to put into Queenstown, about eight miles north. I replied that the ship was for New York, not Queenstown.

At 6pm I went forward again to reason with the men. The yells and language were the worst I have ever heard. Finnigan bared his breast and dared me to shoot, calling me an outrageous name. I raised my pistol at him point-blank, hammer uplifted. Finnigan receded a step or two, and a deadly silence prevailed. Taking advantage of this, I called them to return to duty. They refused, unless I would give them 'watch and watch' and food.

'You will eat when you work!'

This was met with yells, jeers, and 'Kill the old devil!' And, to me, 'Shoot! Shoot! Shoot!'

'I would if I feared you,' I told them. 'But prefer to teach you a lesson. You will regain your senses when hungry.'

'We'll help ourselves when we damn well please!' was Finnigan's answer.

I told them I now considered them pirates, and any man who attempted to come abaft the mainmast would have his brains blown out. This was met with a further brandishing of knives, and a further volley of oaths and hisses.

At dark, fearing that the forecastle hatch might be battened down upon them, the men set a watch of four and four. At midnight, we passed Cape Clear with a six-knot breeze. During the night I walked the deck, the officers relieving one another at the wheel every two hours. There was no sleep. At 7.30am I went forward again, but the same scene was re-enacted.

At noon the breeze freshened, and I ordered, in a voice which could be heard fore and aft, 'Take in the royals.'

The order was met with, 'Go to hell!'

The sails were furled by the officers and boys. The

wind still freshened, and by midnight the ship was tearing along at twelve knots. We managed to lower the topgallant sails to the caps, but still the ship was pitching and burying her forecastle, filling the lee gangway. I never carried sails so hard in my life, but could not lower any more, for we were too light to hoist them again. At 4am the wind moderated, and by eight o'clock it was calm. We reset the topgallants, and I again went forward. They said if they got their breakfast they would turn to.

'Work before food,' I answered.

'Damn you!' was the answer to this.

At 11am we exchanged signals with an Inman steamer, bound east. At noon we tacked southwest, and I went forward with Mr Whitehorn and my pistols to work tacks and sheets, as the men had threatened to throw overboard anyone approaching the forecastle.

During the day several passengers came aft to ask me to feed the men. One or two of the rougher sort went so far as to say that if the request was not complied with, they would supply them themselves.

'I am sorry to hear that,' I said. 'For if they conquer me, after committing the greatest outrages on those you hold most dear, they will batten you down and sink the ship. Then they will take to the boats, and, on being picked up, will say the ship sprang a leak and sank, leaving them the only survivors. These men know that, by marine law, they have subjected themselves to five years in prison, and a fine of five thousand dollars. For them, virtual imprisonment for life. They will kill us all before subjecting themselves to such a penalty. I therefore forbid you to give them food or aid. If you disobey, you are subject to the same penalty to which they are liable. The sympathies you have already shown has protracted this difficulty. Let me see no more. I have now warned you!' Except on two or three, my remarks made a very favourable impression.

To these latter I said, 'Understand me. I have the same authority over you as over my crew, and if I see a possibility of your joining them I will put you in irons.' One still defied me, but after a short tussle Mr Whitehorn and I succeeded in ironing him. None of the other passengers interfered, and they quietly obeyed when I ordered them to leave the decks and go below.

At sunset, clear, and with the ship running eight knots on a wind, I went forward again. As they appeared in a better frame of mind, I said, 'Men! All those who throw their knives overboard and go back to work will be forgiven! Except Finnigan, Casey, and Sweeney.'

This being received with usual hisses, yells, and howls, I went back aft. Fifty-six hours had passed without sleep aft, or food forward. I knew this state of things would have to end very soon, and had not the slightest doubt in my mind that someone would be killed.

At 8pm I ordered Mr Whitehorn to take charge of the deck, and shoot the first man that came abaft the mainmast. I went into the cabin, and passed into the after steerage where the Germans were. In their own language, I pointed out the danger to their loved ones should I be killed.

'Germans,' I continued, 'Most of you have served in the army. As brave men I call upon you to defend your wives and children!'

'Order us, captain, and we will obey!' was their reply.

Reinforced by seventeen of these stalwarts, I armed them with iron bars cut into handy lengths. It was now near midnight and a deathlike stillness prevailed. I was standing at the break of the quarterdeck, Mr Whitehorn nearby. Suddenly, a growl from Wallace drew my attention to the forward gangway, where I saw two men crawling aft with knives in their hands.

'Shall I shoot?' asked Mr Whitehorn.

'No, there are only two.'

'Call the Germans?'

'Not now.' I waited till they got aft as far as the capstan, about twenty feet away, then said. 'Move no farther. Stand, and throw up your arms.' The order was obeyed. 'Walk aft and let me see you. What do you want?'

'Captain, you said you would forgive any who joined you. We are married men, and ask forgiveness.'

'Throw your knives overboard.' They did so. 'Now,

one of you take the wheel, but mark me, if I find any treachery, he will be the first to fall.' I then asked what was happening in the forecastle.

They said Finnigan made them all swear to kill me if I went forward that night, and that he intended to storm the galley at eight bells next morning; that Dutch Bill had said, 'Boys, shall we go back to work?' but had been struck on the head with a serving mallet by Sweeney. 'And was still lying there, captain, when we left to take our watch on deck. Joe and Tom, who relieved us, are willing to join you, too, if we call them. And if you will trust us with arms, we will help bring the rest to terms.'

I sent one of these men forward to tell the other two not to join us yet, but go below as usual. If asked what had become of the first two men, there were to say they had deserted to join the captain. And at the same time, they were told that when I came forward in the morning, at the proper moment, when they could be well heard by all the rest, and at my signal, they were to say, ' Well, boys, here goes my knife,' and throw their weapons overboard.

At five bells (2.30am) the Germans were brought up, the pigpen was placed across the port side as a barricade, and four of them were put behind it, the rest being distributed on the top of the house, and else- where, to prevent the crew from surrounding me. The ladders leading down the steerage were hauled up and the hatches fastened down, to guard against the steerage passengers joining the crew.

At seven bells (3.30am) the two sailors who now had the watch forward were relieved by four others, among whom were Casey and Sweeney, ready to break into the galley and storeroom at dawn.

At 3.45am Mr Whitehorn and I, with Wallace in advance, walked forward on the starboard side. When abreast of the galley, I said, 'Go ahead, Wallace.' When he reached the corner, he gave a deep growl. Knowing Casey and Sweeney were waiting, I proceeded, pistol in hand, to the edge of the house. They both now jumped from behind it, knives raised.

In an instant I levelled my pistol at Casey, while the dog jumped at Sweeney's throat. Casey, seeing his danger, backed to the forecastle scuttle, while the other two watchkeepers yelled 'Jump up, boys! We've got him!!'

With shouts and oaths all now rushed up on deck, determined to finish their work. Some began going round, while others started to clamber over the house to make a flank attack. But now the Germans rose from behind their barricade and felled the ringleaders with their iron bars. Seeing themselves defeated, and me reinforced, the mutineers retreated to the starboard side, forward, where I held them with a levelled pistol.

'Death to the first who advances! Throw your knives overboard.'

Finnigan now spoke up. 'You shall be the first, you damned psalm-singer!'

'Throw your knives and go to work!'

'What guarantee shall we have, captain, that you will not shoot us?' asked one of the men.

'If I do not fear you armed with knives, I certainly will not fear you unarmed, and will give my pistols into the custody of any passenger you name when I see your knives overboard.'

'Will you give us watch and watch, and not prosecute us when we get ashore?'

'Throw your knives and go to work.'

Then one of the men I had primed, said, 'Boys, it's no use! Here goes mine!' With that, one knife after the other went spinning into the sea, just as the sun was rising. A more gratifying sight I never saw than those gleaming blades dropping into the ocean.

After this I discharged my pistols, saying, 'Finnigan, you insulted me, calling me a coward. Now ask my pardon. I take an insult from no man without resenting it – certainly not from you.'

'And I never have, and never will, ask pardon of any man,' he answered.

The spirit of the muscular Christian seized me, and the blow I dealt him sent him headlong down the forecastle, in front of which he had been standing.

'Stand back, men,' I said. 'Whitehorn, bring that fellow up.' Finnigan was found lying at the foot of forecastle ladder, unconscious. A rope was tied around him, and he was hauled up. While Whitehorn was putting the rope around him, he found a knife under his shirt. He called up, and I drew my cutlass, pointing it at Casey and Sweeney. They instantly threw up their arms, asking if I meant to kill them. Mr Whitehorn searched them, and found, as in Finnigan's case, a bowie knife on each: one had it under his jumper, the other in his boot.

'Now, men,' I said, 'You are to jump when you are spoken to, and instead of walking you are to run to obey orders. The last order I gave you, was haul taut the weather mainbrace. Now! Haul taut the weather mainbrace!

With one voice they called, 'Ay, ay, sir!' And from the way they hauled on that brace, I feared they would spring the yard.

'Belay there, men!' I sang out, and then, 'Boy, tell the cook to get the men's coffee ready. Whitehorn, turn them to for holystoning decks.'

By this time Finnigan, under the doctor's care, had recovered from the effects of his trip down the forecastle stairs, and was propped near the break of the poop. I again asked him if he would apologise; he made no reply. I ordered him ironed, and put in the sweatbox. In less than half an hour he cried for mercy, ready to say or do anything. I had him unshackled and brought to the quarterdeck, where all hands were holystoning.

'Men,' I said, 'Listen now to what your recent leader and bully has to say. He who would have led you to the gallows.'

'Captain,' he said, 'I have had enough. To say this does not make a coward of a man who has found his master.'

'Take back your insulting language,' I replied.

'Well, then, captain, whoever calls you a coward is a damned liar.'

'Leave out the "damned". Swearing is prohibited, but if there is any to be done, I have the first privilege. Now down on your knees and holystone.'

'Ay, ay, sir.'

At seven bells all hands were ordered to breakfast. At eight bells they turned to again, scrubbing, stoning, and polishing brasswork with such a will that one would think they'd been promised forty-eight hours leave and a month's pay. All the emigrants were ordered on deck, and 'tween decks were thoroughly cleaned and fumigated, and the men put through a day's work that would make up for lost time. At seven o'clock they were called aft.

'Men,' I said, 'I think we now understand each other.' My heart was further softened when, next Sunday, several of them attended divine worship. For this I allowed them all a glass of grog before dinner.

On a beautiful August morning, the Highland lights hove in sight, and we took a pilot. The men's coffee was served, and I ordered them to reeve the signal halyards fore and aft. This was instantly obeyed, although the men might expect that the signals were for armed assistance. (I had told them at the height of the mutiny that on arrival I would run up signals for the *Harriet Lane*, revenue cutter.)

All hands were ordered into the forecastle, where I joined them with the ship's articles. I told them that I had come to say a few words. I reviewed a part of my forecastle life. How all sailors, myself included, were prey to the sharks ashore. How I, too, had been drugged and sold, bought and robbed. I begged them to break the chains that bound them, and assert the manhood God had given them for a better purpose than to be the slaves of boarding-house keepers and crimps. I told them there was no reason why they should not become officers, captains, or merchants. And drew a picture of a home life with wives and children. Against this, I prophesied the end that would overtake them if they gave way to their passions. I ended with a prayer which brought tears to the eyes of most of these hardened men.

'I leave with you,' said I, 'The articles you signed, or had signed for you. On the back of these are marine laws, with the penalties to which you have subjected yourselves. But I am going to forgive you. I have one request to make, which is that you will not leave the ship until she is moored with rigging stopped up, and you have received from me what little pay is due you. I want you to do this instead of deserting in the usual fashion, thereby allowing landlords, or sailor lawyers, to collect it and cheat you out of most of it. I hope you will do this. For, if what has happened has been the means of converting any of you, I shall count this the most fortunate voyage of my life.' I then went aft.

Shortly after, Finnigan brought the articles to me, saying that he had come to return them and on behalf of the crew to thank me. He said that he knew he had the most to be thankful for, and declared they would all try to be better men.

Abreast of the light-ship, we were taken in tow by the tug. We furled and squared away. At ten we arrived at quarantine, and were passed by the doctor. We discharged our passengers in barges, to be taken to Castle Garden. During this time, news of the mutiny had spread over New York like wildfire. By the time we docked we were besieged by all the runners and sailor-thieves in the city, all expecting a row, in which they would be delighted to take a hand, these villains always considering me a natural enemy who stood between them and their prey.

Much to their astonishment, the men, instead of jumping onto the wharf or overboard, prevented them coming on the ship. It would be impossible to describe the taunts and jeers of these rascals at what they called the 'cowardice' of the crew. But no attention was paid by the men, who were now stowing away hawsers, sweeping decks, and giving the brasswork an extra polish. I paid them off in the cabin.

When about half were paid, the *Kangaroo*, Inman Line, left the dock above us for Liverpool. As usual, our men on deck called to those in the cabin to come up and give three cheers. This was done with a will, and her crew with equal heartiness, returned three cheers for the 'bully *Dreadnought*' whereupon our men gave three cheers for me.

I completed the paying off. And now the men took their seats on the spars, evidently waiting for something. This being reported to me, I went on deck and walked to the capstan. Here they surrounded me, hats in their hands.

Understanding that they wanted a speech, I said, 'I think I know what you wish to say. Your actions speak plainer than words. Let me say that I would trust any of you with my life. I never had, or expect to have, a better set of sailors with me. When I am ready to go to sea again, if any of you want to ship, I shall be glad to take you.'

Then it was three rousing cheers for the 'wild boat of the Atlantic' and their willingness to sail to hell with me. I hoped that they find their families and friends as well as they could wish. With a final 'God bless you, captain,' they left the ship.

Just then Superintendent Kennedy, with a posse of

police, arrived to say that the ship's agent had sent word that the crew, aided by the runners, had attacked the officers and myself.

'There has been a mistake, Kennedy,' I said. 'As you see, the crew are going ashore very peaceably.'

'The mutineers? Shall I arrest them?'

'I would ship with all of them again tomorrow.'

Poor Jack has a hard enough time at the best of it: a prey to plunderers ashore, and the sport and plaything of the elements of the deep, and often at the mercy of officers all too ready to exert to a tyrannous extent the authority they possess. It is little wonder his heart becomes almost dead in his bosom. But let us remember that a little kindness and consideration, joined with firm justice, will often melt that obdurate nature, and make that heart full and warm again.

12. A hurricane and my leg is broken, which I set myself. We lose our rudder, and run for Fayal. My leg finds a doctor after fourteen days but is not made sound for many months. I leave the *Dreadnought*. Final thoughts.

THREE YEARS AFTER the mutiny, I resolved to ship a coloured crew. They did very well during the summer months, but in cold, stormy weather they were worthless, shrinking into themselves so that their jackets would have to be opened to ascertain if they contained human beings. I was sorry for them, but in order to keep their blood in circulation, and to prevent them from falling asleep and freezing on duty, it was necessary for one of the officers to trot them around the decks and stimulate them by a piece of ratline. Each man, too, was supplied with his own piece, to urge the one ahead to a sharper run. This may appear to be cruel, but it is not so cruel as to let them freeze fingers and toes.

February is the worst month to be bound westward from Liverpool to New York. And it was during this month that I was caught in the Devil's Blowhole, a locality named by unanimous consent of all Atlantic sailors, and to be found about latitude 45°, longitude 45°; that is, about two-thirds of the way across from Liverpool. That trip, the barometer indicating heavy weather, at noon our sails were reduced to double-reefs. Packet ships never fully took in sail until the storm was upon them, hence the extraordinary times they made. But by 4pm we were compelled to close reef topsails and furl the mainsail, the smallest canvas the *Dreadnought* ever carried.

The gale steadily increased in fury. The night was a very long one. I was wishing for daylight to put her on the starboard tack as the ship was flying before the wind and sea in the direction opposite to that in which we were bound. I sent for the third officer to watch the steering, while I went forward to see the sails properly handled. Things grew so serious that I intended, for the first time ever, to heave the *Dreadnought* to. The violence of the wind was unimaginable. Up to this time the ship had been well steered, and had gone along dry, but suddenly I felt her careen to port. Looking aft, I saw an immense sea coming on our weather quarter which I knew would sweep the decks. I motioned to the men at the wheel to put the helm up, but they became frightened and put it the wrong way. I called to the boys to run forward and save themselves, while I secured myself under the weather rail, holding onto a couple of iron belaying pins, and straddling the spare foreyard. I felt the shock to the ship as the sea came rushing over, and was then swept away by its irresistible force, buried under water, and thought myself overboard. Then my head came in violent contact with some hard substance and I was rendered unconscious. When my senses returned I was underwater, my head jammed beneath a spar. I closed my mouth to keep from drowning, certain that the crew would soon reach me. Just as I felt I could hold my breath no longer, the ship lurched and allowed the spar to settle, but with sufficient force to again knock me senseless. Regaining consciousness once more I found myself hanging over the lee rail, my head and arms outboard.

The cries from the emigrants, men, women, and children, were heart-rending. I tried to raise my body to prevent myself from being crushed by the floating spars. My left leg I succeeded in raising, but the right one was powerless, it was broken. I was also bleeding from a scalp wound, my left wrist was injured and useless, and I was so exhausted that death had no terror for me. A lee lurch once more brought the monkey rail level with the sea, and I let go my hold from sheer weakness, thinking my time had come.

'Into thy hands, O God, I commit myself,' I uttered. But at this prayer, in the midst of the storm, there was a sudden lull, the water left the deck, and the crew found me and carried me below.

The cabin presented a sad appearance. The skylight had been stove in, and water covered the floor a foot deep. More dead than alive, I was laid upon a sofa and my clothes stripped off. When my right boot and trousers were split down, my leg below the knee revealed a compound oblique fracture, with the skin broken on the inner side. That the femoral artery was punctured was apparent from the bright scarlet colour of the blood I was fast losing. With my remaining strength I ordered a tourniquet applied until I could recover myself, knowing that the hand of God which had snatched me from the deep would not be withdrawn from me now.

As we had no physician on board, and no one who knew how to set a leg, I decided to undertake the task myself, aided by my purser and a couple of men. We tried to force the bones into place while the leg was extended. As there was nothing in the medical books that usually accompany the ship's medicine chest, we did not know that bending the knee would have relaxed the muscles, so a child could have done what was required. After an ineffectual attempt by three strong men to pull the limb into place, I became so exhausted that they desisted. I asked to have a compress applied, to give me time to collect myself. I decided upon amputation. Life was ebbing fast, and now was the time before I became too weak. I had the tourniquet twisted tight, and a knife laid ready. It was going to be necessary for me to perform the operation as no one else would. I gave instructions for the taking up of the arteries, in case I became too weak. But I felt that it was better to die in making the attempt than to die without making it.

At this juncture the second officer, in whom I had much confidence, came below and begged me not to amputate it, and said that as he had had some hospital practice, he could bandage the limb to stop the bleeding. He said that he had fallen from the main-topgallant yard of the *Benjamin Adams* and broken both legs, which he now showed me, and which were as crooked as ram's horns. He said that we were in the track of the steamers, which always carried surgeons, and might fall in with one at any time.

As the weather was moderating, I took his advice, and my leg was laid in a V-shaped box, while I was wedged on the sofa to keep from rolling. I could now take stock of the ship. We lost our rudder, and were at the mercy of the waves, but the weather had further moderated, and the morning sun rose with a light breeze. I sent for the carpenter to instruct him how to fit a jury rudder. I found that he had been killed the day previous but his death had been concealed from me. I gave the instructions to others, and, at the same time, orders to proceed on the wind for Fayal in the Azores, about three hundred and sixty miles away

Another day passed, and at midnight the jury rudder

was ready to be shipped. Tackles were hooked from the fore and main yards, but it had scarcely been hoisted over the rail, when the straps parted and the whole apparatus dropped overboard and was lost. This nearly drove me frantic.

Another four days passed. Sleep was a stranger to me, narcotics seemed to excite instead of quieting me. My diet was tea and toast, instead of the nourishing food which I should have taken. The leg was kept cool by constant applications of wet cloths. I had excellent nursing from the stewardess, and from the purser. The latter had been with me on several voyages, and I had taught him some navigation. He could mark the ship's position, and bring it to me for verification.

On the fifth morning a Frenchman hove into sight. She answered our signals of distress by sending over a boat with the chief officer. They, too, had no doctor on board. I could not prevail upon him to tow us in but nor could he induce me to leave the ship although he expected to be in Bordeaux in four days. He kindly agreed to take a hawser and turn our ship's head southward, when, with sails properly trimmed, we might make Fayal.

From nine in the morning until three in the afternoon, we undertook to run him a line, but in vain. There is no doubt this was bad seamanship, for at times the Frenchman would pass so close a man could have jumped on board. I sent for the second mate and our

Herculean boatswain, and ordered the former to take charge of the ship, and the latter to support him. I had no confidence in my first officer. My whole trouble I believed had been caused by his incompetence, through his failure to have the sails properly handled, which had made it necessary for me to leave the quarterdeck. The boatswain went into the boat with a fresh crew and reached the French ship, while the second mate paid out a line with an attached hawser. The Frenchman hauled in, but now the hawser kinked, and the line parted.

As night was closing in the Frenchman sent his boat alongside with his compliments, but regretted that he would have to leave me, as he could waste no more time. I refused again to go on board his ship but wrote letters home, and to our agents in New York and Liverpool. These he promised to post.

With the wind still fresh, another jury rudder was begun. This was successful, and we backed on a southerly course at the average of three and a half knots. A light wind favoured us and we arrived at Fayal on the evening of the fourteenth day after the accident.

My leg was in a shocking condition, my body covered with bed sores, my face shrunken beyond recognition. As soon as we anchored, Mr Samuel Dabney came alongside, with the assuring words that though quarantine laws forbade his boarding after sundown, he would be back next morning with a doctor. I found that night the longest since the accident. I had not slept during the entire fourteen days, at least, I had never lost consciousness of my pain, or been free of mental anxiety. A further great anxiety now was the enormous cost that would be incurred in repairing her. As there was no dry dock, she would have to be hove down, which would necessitate discharging the cargo. There was also the cost of maintaining, or forwarding, the passengers. I felt there would be little left of the ship after her debts were paid. But I also matured a plan to avoid this, should I live to have it executed.

Early next morning I was placed on a high-sided stretcher and taken to the gangway, where a whip from the main yard lowered me over the side. The wails of the warm-hearted emigrants were heart-rending. They had never expected to see me alive again.

Once on shore, although among friends, I pulled my cap over my face to hide it from the curious eyes of the Portuguese. My stretcher was carried on the shoulders of natives to the hotel. Captain Winslow was on the island waiting to take command of the *Kearsarge*, also Captain and Mrs Grey. These, with an American dentist and his wife, vied with one another to alleviate my suffering. I gained strength so rapidly that in two weeks I was ready to be operated upon. The doctors of Fayal, two in number, knew little of modern surgical practice, amputation being their hobby. To this I objected, for a one-legged sailor is doomed to shore service, though a one-armed one, with a steel auxiliary, is still sometimes seen on shipboard.

As for the *Dreadnought*, after survey by various underwriters' agents, I was told the ship would have to be stripped, and hove down. I would not accept this, suggesting she should be trimmed by the head to bring up her sternpost, when there could be fitted a new rudder cradle of my devising, and a rudder, even though this new rudder would be five feet shorter than the old one. This would save enormous expense and delay. Mr Dabney agreed it could be done, and had it executed against the protests of the agents, who declared that the ship would not be seaworthy. I said that I would assume the responsibility, as I intended to go home in the *Dreadnought* – leg and all.

Some shipmasters are all too ready to take advice from agents in foreign ports, happy to shift their responsibility upon others. They also make the sad mistake of giving up their command to pilots. The pilot's duty is only to indicate the courses to be steered, but he will obligingly takes command if the captain desires or allows it.

On our fourteenth day I was ready for the doctor to draw my leg, now two inches shorter than the other. The bedstead was secured by shores and braces, head and foot. My thigh was fastened by a sheet to the headpost, and my foot secured by a towel to a tackle hooked to a strap, which was held by a beam outside the window casement. Chloroform was applied, and three of my sailors hauled upon the tackle. This was the kind of bonesetting practised then – but nor was I any more skilfully treated later on. A part of my heel had to be taken off on account of gangrene. The heel had also dropped out of position, and forced a point of bone through the flesh that looked like a large front tooth. This, after what I had suffered in the past forty days, nearly deprived me of my courage.

We were, however, in constant expectation of the arrival of the *Kearsarge*, which, I knew, carried an American surgeon. But when she did arrive, all he was ready to do was to amputate. This I would not listen to. He eventually advised me to wait until I reached home, saying another month of such treatment as I had already received would kill me. He packed my leg, and I was put on board the *Dreadnought* after being ashore fifty-two days. In this state I arrived in New York.

Dr Ayers, of Brooklyn, and Dr Stone, of New York, immediately cut off part of the exposed bone, placed it in position, and held it by wire passed through holes bored in the bones, and then lashed. My convalescence was slow, and I was not out of bed till November. Twenty-three years have since passed, and my leg, strange to say, is now as long as its fellow, and just as strong, nor is it affected by changes in the weather. The Achilles tendon has somewhat too close a hold upon the heel, causing me at times to limp, but so slightly as to be hardly perceptible. I hope I have not tired the reader with this history, but present it as affording an illustration of the endurance of which the human body is capable when it has a firm willpower.

In ending, I would like to say something about boys who crave a sea life. A young fellow in this position knows little of the hardships he will have to endure. He is kicked and cuffed by all on board. He is last to turn in, and is expected to be the first out. He has last chance at the mess-kid. He is sometimes made to leave his sleep to light some brute's pipe. Every Saturday he has to slush down the masts, and, in tarring, his job is to tar down the light stays. Sailors have an idea that the rougher a boy is treated the better man he will make.

However, there are some incorrigible young rascals who are better at sea than ashore. While it is kill or cure, if a boy is bright and daring, can stand the hard usage, is not carried off by a malignant fever, does not fall from aloft and become crippled, or does not lose his life by shipwreck, and can pass through the degrading influences of the forecastle, he may make master of a ship. If his lucky star clings to him in the selection of a wife, he will make a good citizen. However, the chances against are a thousand to one. And if he does arrive at command, what then? If he loses his ship, although it may not be through any want of skill or care, he suffers a black mark and perhaps may never get another vessel as captain. If his ship sinks under him and lives are lost, he is looked upon as a coward for not going down with it, though he may be the bravest of the brave.

Boys, look in the graveyards and read the tombstones. Then tell me how many sailors are buried there. Has it ever occurred to you how few die natural deaths?

Notes

1. Lubbock, Basil, *The Western Ocean Packets* (Glasgow, 1925).
2. Birch, H Clarkson, *An Old Sailor's Yarn* (Ipswich, 1914), p.109.
3. Admiral W H Smyth, *The Sailor's Word Book* (London, 1867), p.223.
4. Taylor, William, ed W P Strickland, *Seven Years Street Preaching in San Francisco* (New York & London, 1875), pp.236-7.
5. McCulloch, John Herries, *A Million Miles in Sail* (Hurst and Blackett, Paternoster Library, nd), p.42.
6. Domville-Fife, Charles W, *Square Rigger Days: Autobiographies of Sail* (Barnsley, 2007).
7. Armstrong, Warren, *Freedom of the Seas* (Jarrolds, London, nd [*c.*1943]), p.82.
8. Williams, Frederick B, *On Many Seas* (New York & London, 1897).
9. Applejack, a spirit distilled from apples, similar to apple or cider brandy.
10. Able seaman.
11. Scoured with soft sandstone to clean them.
12. Nathaniel Bowditch's *The New American Practical Navigator*, the standard handbook of navigation, first published in 1802.
13. Turkish tobacco pipe.
14. Waterproof hat.
15. Osceola (born Billy Powell, 1804-38) was a leader of the Seminoles in Florida. He was of mixed English, Scottish, Irish and Creek Native American descent, and married an African-American woman.

SEAFARERS' VOICES

A new series of seafaring memoirs

This new series, Seafarers' Voices, presents a set of abridged and highly readable first-hand accounts of maritime voyaging in the age of sail, which describe life at sea from different viewpoints – naval, mercantile, officer and lower deck, men and women – and cover the years 1700 to the 1900s, from the end of the Mediterranean galleys, through the classic age of sail to the coming of the steamship. Published in chronological order, these memoirs unveil the extraordinary and unfamiliar world of our seafaring ancestors and show how they adapted to the ever-demanding and ever-changing world of ships and the sea, both at war and at peace.

The first titles in the series

For more details visit our website
www.seaforthpublishing.com